Tales of Hope and Hilarity
for a Sandwiched Generation

Family Squeeze

Phil Callaway

MULTNOMAH
BOOKS

FAMILY SQUEEZE

PUBLISHED BY MULTNOMAH BOOKS
12265 Oracle Boulevard, Suite 200
Colorado Springs, Colorado 80921
A division of Random House Inc.

All Scripture quotations, unless otherwise indicated, are taken from the Holy Bible, New International Version®. NIV®. Copyright © 1973, 1978, 1984 by International Bible Society. Used by permission of Zondervan Publishing House. All rights reserved. Scripture quotations marked (NLT) are taken from the Holy Bible, New Living Translation, © 1996, 2004. Used by permission of Tyndale House Publishers, Inc., Wheaton, Illinois 60189. All rights reserved. Scripture quotations marked (Phillips) are taken from The New Testament in Modern English © 1958, 1960 by J. B. Phillips. Scripture quotations marked KJV are taken from the King James Version.

ISBN: 978-1-59052-916-4

Library of Congress Cataloging-in-Publication Data
Callaway, Phil, 1961–
    Family squeeze : tales of hope and hilarity for a sandwiched generation / Phil
Callaway. — 1st ed.
        p. cm.
    Includes bibliographical references.
    ISBN 978-1-59052-916-4
    1. Family—Religious aspects—Christianity. 2. Intergenerational relations—Religious aspects—Christianity. 3. Parenting—Religious aspects—Christianity. 4. Aging parents—Care—Religious aspects—Christianity. I. Title.
    BT707.7.C36 2008
    242—dc22

                                            2007037987

Printed in the United States of America
2008—First Edition

10 9 8 7 6 5 4 3 2 1

SPECIAL SALES
Most WaterBrook Multnomah books are available in special quantity discounts when purchased in bulk by corporations, organizations, and special interest groups. Custom imprinting or excerpting can also be done to fit special needs. For information, please e-mail SpecialMarkets @WaterBrookPress.com or call 1-800-603-7051.

"Phil has done it again: made us laugh and cry reading just one page of this magical, wonderful book! The best of life is always captured by Phil Callaway's words, and he inspires us all to live a life worthy of passing on to our families and friends. He brings out the best in humankind, all while making us laugh out loud."

—BILL AND PAM FARREL, authors of *Men Are Like Waffles,
Women Are Like Spaghetti*

"I don't know of anyone else who makes me laugh out loud, and then within moments, finds a way to touch the deep parts of my heart. Maybe it's because I helped care for my parents the last ten years of their lives, or maybe it's just that our journeys really are much more similar than we realize. Whatever the case, *Family Squeeze* was particularly timely for me. Phil has a knack for helping us remember God's presence in the hardest seasons of life, and he provides a generous dose of humor, lest we get lost in the maze of self-absorption."

—STEVE GREEN, Dove Award–winning musical artist
and author

"This book blindsided me big time and moved me profoundly. A masterful, well-crafted manual filled with phenomenal advice and fall-down funny stories, this book has been a life-changer for my wife and me. If you're caught in the squeeze of two generations, Phil delivers life-saving counsel to help you navigate the darkness. In implementing the wisdom of this book, my lost joy has come home. The power of this book is in the fact that Callaway has already been where I am going! Thank God for his warm, wise words that illuminate the unknown path ahead."

—MIKE SILVA, evangelist and author of *Would You Like
Fries with That?*

"I loved reading this book. *Family Squeeze* is funny; VERY FUNNY and seriously honest. I'm grateful that Phil has transparently shared his life so we baby boomers could be reminded how to leave footsteps worth following."

> —BRIAN DOERKSEN, worship leader and author of "Come, Now Is the Time" and "Faithful One"

"I laughed and cried and identified wholly as I read *Family Squeeze*. Phil Callaway has the gift of using gentle humor to convey powerful truth; in this case that family is infinitely worth loving, however difficult the moment, and that God's grace and strength are the hope that carries us through each day. A must-read for every parent caught in midlife crisis between teenage hormones and aging parents."

> —JEANETTE WINDLE, author of *Crossfire* and *Firestorm*

"I commend to you the sentiments expressed in this volume, not only because we need them and because Phil wrote them, but more importantly because he and Ramona live the grace so humorously articulated here. I'm already planning to move in with them when I retire."

> —TIM CALLAWAY, columnist, pastor, and brother to Phil

"Phil Callaway's books are not just a pleasure to savor, like eating a perfectly ripe pear. They are full of firm insights that give grace for the daily race, especially when the journey is hard. I loved *Family Squeeze*. If your life is full of children, parents, and everything in between, you'll love this book too."

> —ELLEN VAUGHN, *New York Times* bestselling author of *It's All About Him* and *Time Peace*

Family
Squeeze

To my loving siblings, Dave, Dan, Tim, and Ruth,
who tell people that their younger brother
is a successful court stenographer.

❧

And to my children, from their number one fan,
who anticipates the day they discover that
the volume control also goes left.

CONTENTS

Introduction
Shotgun Memories

*Snatching the eternal out of the desperately fleeting
is the great magic trick of human existence.*

TENNESSEE WILLIAMS

A few years back, when my forehead was covered by hair, I agreed to write a column called "Family Matters" for *Servant* magazine. It was a daunting task for a young father and one for which I feel underqualified to this day. Staring down the barrel of that first deadline, I whined to my wife, Ramona, about the stress of it all. "I can't do it," I said. "Look at me. I'm an imperfect dad. I get mad at my kids. I used to slide hamsters down banisters when I was a child. I argue with my wife sometimes."

She laughed. "So write about it," she said. "Tell stories. Tell us you feel like a failure sometimes. And tell us there's hope."

"But I'm no Dr. Dobson," I protested.

"I know," she sighed, stabbing at a potato in the sink. "He has money."

The next day I sat at my desk, wondering what to write. The job was too big for me, so I pushed my chair back and got on my knees to pray. Then I wrote "Shotgun Memories," the story of a hunting trip gone right. With five children and a to-do list taller than me, my dad somehow managed to throw a shotgun into our '62 Meteor and invest a Saturday in his youngest son. A decade later we fishtailed down those same dusty roads with the same shotgun in the backseat. But this time it would serve a different purpose. This time Dad handed it to a farmer, trading it in on my very first car. The shotgun was an emblem, of course, of a father who took time for me.

Animal rights activists got hold of my article and twisted it. They didn't appreciate my hunting or my work with hamsters. But kind letters began arriving too. People stopped me on the street. One said, "Great article! I'll never forget you, Bill." The farmer even called: "Phil," he drawled, "I want you to have that shotgun." I thanked him repeatedly, surprised that he had been so utterly blessed by the article that he was offering me the precious shotgun as a gift. I couldn't stop thanking him.

"How does two hundred bucks sound?" he asked.

I coughed. "Not very good," I said. After all, we hardly had two quarters to rub together in those days. Where would I ever come up with two hundred bucks?

Our children were three, two, and almost one at the time. (We had them so fast the anesthetic from the first birth was still working for the third.) They came along with no instruction manuals, no mute buttons, and no guarantees. They slimed doorknobs, left pointy toys on the stairway, and yowled long into the night. We were underqualified for the task, plus we were terrified. What if they turned out to be…well, what if they turned out to be like me? And so we did the only thing we knew to do: We got down on our knees and prayed.

A surprising thing happened: We found that we loved parenting (after the kids were asleep, and sometimes when they were awake). Sure, the children screamed, put jam sandwiches in the VCR, and turned dinnertime into a full-contact sport. But we loved these precious, sticky-faced gifts. We held them tightly, read to them often, and gave them back to God each night.

Our children are teenagers now. They come with a whole new set of challenges. Sometimes it's hard to decide if growing pains are something they have or something they are. Once again, we're in over our heads, so we get down on our knees.

And now a whole new challenge has entered our lives: aging parents. Once again I find myself looking for an instruction manual, a mute button, and some guarantees.

Instead, I have discovered that we are not alone. That a zillion other baby boomers are experiencing a stretch of time when the answers grow quiet and the questions slither in like the neighbor's cat every time you open the door:

- How do we honor our aging parents without guilt while raising our children without regret?
- How do we retain our sanity in the midst of so much change (assuming we were sane in the first place)?
- Is it possible to live without the stress, remorse, and anxiety that so many lug around with them?
- How do I learn to laugh so that when I retire all my wrinkles will be in the right places?
- And who said I'm having a midlife crisis? I've wanted a red convertible since third grade.

One night I sneaked up behind Ramona as she was stabbing potatoes again (be careful when you do this) and asked her if I should write about these things. She said, "Yeah, we need the money." No, she didn't. She said, "Sure. But we're tired, so make us laugh. And tell us there's hope, too. Oh, and while you're at it, would you fix the dishwasher?"

What follows are stories of hope and hilarity amid the turbulence and splendor of what I've come to call the Middle Ages. I'll admit that I often felt ill equipped for the task while writing this book. But then I was reminded that God seldom gives us anything we aren't to share with others, that nothing worthwhile I've ever accomplished didn't initially scare me half to death, and that God often uses the timid and trembling to do His work. I guess it's because we know we can't do it on our own. And when good things happen, we never doubt who deserves the credit.

I pray this book will meet you where you are but not leave you there. I pray that you'll savor these stories and find some help here too.

Sometimes, as I was writing, I found myself looking at a shotgun that hangs above my study door. It's a lifelong reminder of a father's love for me. A reminder that time is ticking. That the best retirement investment in all the world is memories. And it's a reminder that sometimes writers strike it rich. After all, I sold my very first article to another magazine for two hundred bucks and bought that shotgun.

Grandma's Baby

*It's not easy taking my problems one
at a time when they refuse to get in line.*

ASHLEIGH BRILLIANT

❦

*How far you go in life depends on being tender with
the young, compassionate with the aged, sympathetic with
the striving, and tolerant of the weak and strong—because
someday you will have been all of these.*

GEORGE WASHINGTON CARVER

One of the most profound prayers I have ever prayed is "Help!" Sometimes it's as simple as "Help, I cannot find my left shoe." Or "Help, I cannot find my passport, and I'm second in line." But lately the prayer has been increasingly desperate, uttered through clenched teeth, because I feel like a pair of wet swim shorts about to be squeezed through one of those ancient wringer washing machines.

On my forty-fourth birthday—the same day Mick Jagger turned sixty-three—I dragged myself out of bed to take my younger son golfing. I could think of no better reason to get up and face old age.

As we strolled the course together, whacking a little white ball and sometimes kicking it, Jeff informed me that he was thinking of buying a Ford Mustang and dating a pretty girl. I threw him a Charles Manson look and said I was considering pushing him in the creek. The child lives life like he golfs: carefully planning his attack, then lunging at things and whapping them.

After tallying our scores, we drove to visit my mother, who needs me, among other things, to finish sentences for her. They don't prepare you for this in college. You learn of ancient languages and philosophy, but there's no course on what to do when your mother insists that your son's iPod is her hearing aid.

As we visit, Mom hands me her "baby"—a blanket scrunched, twisted, and spilled upon by numerous patrons of the long-term care facility where she now resides. Few know that she was once the author of many books, adored by her children and a dozen women who still call her Mom and mentor. The years have been kind to her relatively unwrinkled face, but her memories are distant now, her mind perpetually fuzzy, frantic at times, like she knows things I don't and wonders if she should burden me with them.

She leans forward, eager to ask me something. "Is your wife—you know—pregnant?"

Jeff snorts.

"No, Mom, not that I know of."

"Did the divorce go through?" It is one of her longer sentences.

I shake my head and smile. I, her lastborn son, who has been married to his high school sweetheart since the advent of disco.

While nursing Mom's bundle of blankets, I try to lighten the air with chatter. I tell her of our golf game, of my birthday, which we will celebrate at lunch tomorrow, just the two of us. She is focused on my bald spot now and is holding hands with Jeff.

The boy loves his grandma; loved to sit on her lap as she read to him when he was toddling. But he never saw the story ending this way. How quickly his face changes from grin to grimace when we visit her. He leans forward and drapes his other arm across her shoulder.

I am holding the baby with one hand and a steaming cup of herbal tea with the other when my cell phone begins playing the "Hallelujah Chorus." Setting the teacup on a table, I flip the phone open to find things further complicated. Though the connection is bad, I can hear my wife's desperate voice:

"Phil," she sobs, "it's Steve. He—"

And the phone goes dead.

Handing the baby to Jeff, I sprint for the nearest landline, praying my favorite prayer. My mind races to keep up with my pulse.

Steve, the eldest of our three teens, is on a trip overseas, smack-dab in the middle of one of the world's hot spots. My nightmares of late have been plagued by images of his demise. I dare not think the worst, but now it appears to be upon us. Down the hallway around the corner, I grab the phone but hesitate before dialing.

I suppose this day is a microcosm of our lives the past few years. Dreaming. Dreading. Laughing. Answering the phone a little less eagerly. We are parenting two generations now, wedged between the demands of elderly dependents and energetic teens—neither of whom think you know very much. I attend to my duties begrudgingly at times. I am husband, father, and son. But my résumé also includes psychiatrist, doctor, advisor, and Power of Attorney—which, I assure you, does not come with a lawyer's salary. I feel like a rookie juggler who has been put in charge of ticket sales, concessions, and training the animals too.

Years ago a scholarship sales representative sat us down to threaten us with how much it would cost our kids to go to college. He didn't mention the price of caring for our parents.

Most weekends find me traveling near and far helping audiences laugh, telling them where the joy comes from. Yet in those moments of stark honesty I must admit that my stiff upper lip quivers sometimes, that lurking just beneath the smile is a growing sadness. It's the kind of sadness you feel watching the last sunset of fall, knowing that winter is about to stagger in on you.

I dial the number, expecting the worst. The phone rings, and Ramona picks it up. She is more composed now. "I'm sorry," she says. "It's just that…Steve called. He has malaria. Sorry, I sort of lost it."

I am elated. My son has malaria! If I were any good at dancing, I'd break into the salsa right now.

Jeff is talking with Grandma when I return, curling her hands in both of his. Already he has learned one of the secrets to a rich life: In dark times, give off light.

"Everything's fine," I tell him. "Steve just has malaria."

He squints at me like I've lost my mind. And since Grandma has lost her hearing, he quietly shares what she's been saying to him.

"So you've been stealing her money, eh?" I laugh. "What money?"

The boy is strong but tender, with eager eyes and a hunger for life. But sometimes I wonder if he's seeing too much of it, if what might be coming scares him. Sometimes I want to shield my children from life. Yet what do you do? Take them only to movies with happy endings? Never buy them a puppy? At least if your heart gets broken, you'll know you have one.

Out in the car, I ponder this journey we've been on the last few glorious and frantic years. I may not know much, but I do know this: We will walk this road together. I have no idea where it will take us, but just as my parents took time for me, I will take time for them. As surely as childhood is about family, old age is family time too.

I think of a friend's advice: *Right foot, left foot, breathe.* "Help," I mutter. "I'm squeezed between my parents and my kids."

And God speaks with words from my younger son, this gift of God who at times I feel like throttling. "So Mom is a basket case, Grandma's in the loony bin, and Steve has malaria. Other than that, things aren't bad. Happy birthday, Dad."

When he talks like this, I want to lock him in a bear hug.

"It could be worse," I say. "My youngest son could start dating."

"Maybe," he laughs, cupping his hand out the window against the oncoming wind.

His laugh has me thinking I can muster the courage to face a birthday cake with forty-four lit candles. Maybe climb out of bed again tomorrow and move my feet, one at a time.

Extreme Makeover

Retirement at sixty-five is ridiculous.
When I was sixty-five I still had pimples.

GEORGE BURNS, WHEN HE WAS ONE HUNDRED

❧

"Honor your father and mother"—which is the first com-
mandment with a promise—"that it may go well with you
and that you may enjoy long life on the earth."

EPHESIANS 6:2–3

Somewhere back in the last century, my siblings and I began to face the fact that our parents were aging. We noticed this when we caught Dad backing his Ford Tempo out of the driveway without the aid of mirrors, only to park the car in the flower bed. Sometimes he drove like an Indy racer, and other times farmers on combines would pull out to pass him.

It was as if my once-athletic father, who had been the picture of good health until just after retirement, was kidnapped by those make-over guys on ABC and kept in a room while they dyed his hair, wrinkled his face, and forced him to push a cane around for the rest of his life.

In a matter of months, my dynamic dad seemed to officially enter old age, waving a sad farewell to baseball with the grandkids and his patriarchal role at family reunions. Instead, he would tire easily, find a sofa, and doze off. I wasn't sure I had ever seen my father cry, but now the tears came readily as he sat in my green leather chair—the tiger of my youth, now panting under a shade tree.

Ramona and I talked about aging a lot in those days, wondering what role, if any, we should play in Mom and Dad's lives. Of their five children, I lived the closest, just a ten-minute stroll from their house— the perfect distance when we needed baby-sitting services. But there came a day when Mom and Dad no longer accepted the assignments as eagerly, and when they did, they didn't move quickly enough to chase the kids from poisonous plants or fast-moving buses. I joked with them about it, saying it's a good thing we don't bear children in our eighties; we'd likely fold the strollers before removing the kids.

Though their house was tiny, for them it had grown in size. My mother, who had waged a successful battle with dust and dirt her entire life, finally waved the white flag. Their lawn, once carefully groomed, now required one of those farmer's combines, not a mower. Through faint tears Dad admitted that things were too big for him now. The only part of the house that was too small was the medicine cabinet. He talked of moving into a seniors' lodge, where they would experience measured independence but no room for company.

"We want *life* around us," he confessed. "Old people are like manure. Spread 'em around and they do some good. Pile them together too long and things start to stink."

I went to peers for advice. Those who had been through it were bursting with compassion. A few had regrets. The ones with the most advice and the strongest opinions hadn't traveled this road before. But we all agreed on one thing: 100 percent of living people are aging. And not since the dash on Methuselah's tombstone signaled 969 years have people lived so long.

When my parents were born, less than one in twenty-five lived long enough to blow out sixty-five candles.[1] Today, it seems six out of every four do. (Also, 73 percent of the people attending a Rolling Stones concert receive a senior's discount.) To complicate things further, most of us have two parents and two parents-in-law, so the odds are pretty good that we will carry some responsibility for a dependent parent.

We are also having children later in life. When I was born, my parents were old. So old that I was born in a nursing home. My father had his first heart attack playing peekaboo with me. They were paying for my diapers with pension checks. But this was not the norm. In 1970, the average age of a first-time American mother was 21.4 years.[2] Today, that number has risen to almost twenty-five years[3] (it is twenty-nine in Switzerland).[4] Studies conducted in the United States and Canada conclude that close to 30 percent of women between forty-five and sixty-four are supporting unmarried children and elderly parents at the same time.[5] In the UK 24 percent of adults aged between forty-five and sixty-four are caregivers.[6] The "Me" generation suddenly has to think of others.

One day Ramona asked me a question that I did not appreciate, one that annoyed me to no end: How will we want to be treated when we're my parents' age? She believed that we should do unto them as we would have our children do unto us. I asked her where she could possibly find *that* in the Bible.

She mentioned, among other things, the Old and New Testaments, then suggested I read one of the Ten Commandments. I hate it when she does this. In reading the words again, I discovered that eight of the commandments begin with the words *Do not.* Or, if you read the latest translation, "Hey! Enough with…" Only two of the ten are *Dos,* and this is one: "Honor your father and your mother." The command is not a sin to shun, but a virtue to shoot for. And as far as I can tell, the command does not end at high school graduation. It continues throughout life.

But what does this honoring mean? When you're barely out of diapers, honoring your parents includes obeying them and not smashing china. When you're out of their home, this honor is a trickier thing, but surely it still includes not smashing their china when you visit and being the kind of person who makes a parent of any age say with an upturned grin, "Hey, that's my kid."

Like it or not, we live in a culture that has, for the most part, managed to erase the elderly from our minds and consciences. They are an invisible lot, relegated to nursing homes and hospitals, their convenient disappearance seldom the topic of polite conversation. You may recall this bumper sticker: "Support bingo. Keep Grandma off the streets." I smile when I see it, but I also wonder what we miss by stowing Grandma away.

One day Ramona came to me with a suggestion that I couldn't believe. "Where do you find *that* in the Bible?" I asked.

"Just about everywhere," she said.

"But there's no way it will work," I protested.

"I think it will," she said.

Harry just spent a fortune on a high-definition TV.
Turns out he has low-definition eyes.

3

Suite Memories

Blessed are the young,
for they shall inherit the National Debt.

HERBERT HOOVER

My father's addiction to ice cream started when he quit smoking cigarettes almost fifty years ago. It added years to his life, he claims, but has been just about as expensive.

(I once joked with Dad that he should have kept all the money he saved by not smoking and drinking—we could have taken it to a casino and tried to win some more. I mentioned this once while speaking and received a very short letter WRITTEN IN ALL CAPS with lots of exclamation points. Sadly, the person forgot to sign it, so I couldn't tell him I was kidding.)

If you invited Dad to dinner and asked if he'd like a little ice cream, he would shake his head. "No," he'd say. "I'd like *a lot* of ice cream." And so we are meeting at an ice cream shop this windy autumn afternoon. It's the ideal spot to speak of something that's been on my mind for a while.

Dad and Mom pull up in their hunter green Ford Tempo. Ramona and I watch as they labor to untangle themselves from the cramped front seat. They aren't as spry as they were ten years ago—or six months ago, for that matter.

My father orders a large vanilla cone roofed in chocolate and feigns reluctance as I pull out my wallet. Mom's tastes are much simpler: hot water with milk and honey, something I've seen her drink a hundred times but never had the nerve to try myself. They are holding hands as she takes dainty sips from the cup, her smile almost concealing the worry wrinkles tugging at her brow.

Conversation comes easily. The fall colors are particularly vibrant this year, says Dad. It reminds them both of their hometown. The laughter comes too. Something a grandchild said. Dad has always loved making us laugh, so he puts his nose in the ice cream like a little kid.

Finally there is a lull in the conversation, and I clear my throat, wondering how they'll take to our idea. "Would you like to be in on our little building project?" I ask.

Dad wipes the ice cream from his nose. "What are you building?"

"A house. We plan to start in the spring. We'd like to include a small suite in it for you."

Their eyes grow wide. Dad squeezes Mom's hand. Bright smiles, long on vacation, quickly return. I haven't seen them this excited since they last had their corns removed.

Mom asks Ramona, "What do you think?"

She smiles. "It was my idea," she says.

"We'll only need one bedroom," Dad promises, his eyes dancing.

"I'll have to see a marriage license before you move in," I tell him.

We all lean forward as I pull out some drawings. The suite will be small but comfortable. Outside the bedroom is a bathroom and laundry. The kitchen is adequate, the dining room is small, and the living room is large enough for some furniture, a fireplace, and a sofa bed. "You can use it for company," I suggest.

"Or arguments," says Mom.

The two are arm in arm now. Uncomfortable with the tears running down their cheeks, I try to joke. "We're putting big padlocks on all the doors and extra soundproofing in the walls," I say. "Go ahead and argue."

"Can we play loud music?" asks Dad.

"You can take up the bagpipes if you like."

๑๑

A few people thought we had lost our minds, but our friends were unanimously supportive. Their responses ranged from envy to incredulity. "My parents wouldn't live with us if a tornado leveled their place," joked one. "Maybe during the millennial kingdom when the lion lies down with the lamb."

I was telling another friend that my parents would be living thirty feet from us, and he looked at me like I'd just ordered him off a cliff. "I took my parents to the airport this morning," he said. "Their flight leaves tomorrow."

Others asked how it would work. We didn't know.

One said, "I hope we can do the same one day. Congratulations!"

I told him, "Don't congratulate me. I have a doctorate in selfishness, but every once in a while I experience a momentary lapse."

๑๑

Eleven months later the house was complete, and we set about making it a home. It took a three-hour yard sale one Saturday to sell the stuff my parents had spent a lifetime gathering. "Junk," Dad insisted, but I could tell he had trouble letting some of it go.

Those were golden times. Every week or two we joined them on their patio, sipping iced tea and gazing west across fields finally unlocked from the frosts of winter. In the distance, mountain peaks poked above the horizon. A row of gnarled pines cast long shadows where Mom helped us plant a garden and Dad helped us paint a fence. They assisted with our fledgling book business, with proofreading and mailing, offering topical advice, busy with things they loved.

And every night without fail, Jeff would tap on their door and go in for a good-night hug. Rachael loved reading to them. Steve opted to watch hockey with his grandpa on Saturday nights. I snapped pictures of the two of them eating ice cream and pizza—usually in that order. Sometimes Ramona and I would eavesdrop, but mostly we'd slip out, leaving the five of them together. We talked of never returning, and wondered if they'd really miss us at all.

We had no idea what lay ahead, so we did the only thing we knew to do: took that next step, believing it to be the right one.

4

The Teenagers Are Coming

Never lend your car to anyone
to whom you have given birth.
ERMA BOMBECK

A long about the time we took on boarders, Ramona and I awakened to the fact that our children had become teenagers. Not that they were always easy to have around before, but they were now showing more of a penchant for the irrational, which was summed up well years ago in a book title: *Get Out of My Life, but First Could You Drive Me and Cheryl to the Mall?*

It seemed hardly a week ago that they were in the springtime of life. Now it was more like summer—too much heat and late nights, too much energy and growth. I said to my wife one morning, "Isn't God wise and good? He gave us twelve years to develop a love for our dear little children so we wouldn't lock them in the trunk and swallow the keys when they became teenagers."

My first introduction to teens—apart from being one myself—was when a teenage girl began baby-sitting our kids. We paid her to act like an adult so we could go out and act like teenagers. We also paid her five bucks an hour to eat twenty bucks' worth of our food and watch our movies while she did her homework.

From the day they are born, children have one thing in mind: becoming teenagers and taking over the planet. They want us grownups out of the way. They make fun of our hairstyle (if we are lucky enough to have one), spend our money, crash our car, and eat our lunch. They even stop laughing at our jokes.

Someone asked me the other day what I do. "I'll tell you what I do," I said. "I follow teenagers around the house. I shut lights off. I close fridge doors." It's a full-time job.

Here are a few things I am waiting to hear my teenagers say. I believe I would die of heart failure if they made any two of these statements in the same evening:

- Who needs to eat out? Let me make something.
- Dad, I sure could use a little advice.
- We won't need the car—we're walking.
- There's nothing to eat around here. I'll go buy something.
- We don't do anything as a family anymore.
- You relax, I'll do the dishes.
- New movies aren't cool. Let's watch something old.
- Hey, I've been on the phone a lot. Why don't I pay the phone bill this month?
- Is my music bothering you?
- This is my room, but it's your house.
- Well, lookie there! It's 10 p.m.! I'd better go to bed!

If you are the parent of a teenager, here is something you need to tell yourself each and every day. Apart from selling mittens to South Africans, parenting teenagers is the world's toughest job, so go easy on yourself. Do not compare yourself with other parents who sit in church looking happy and well organized. Chances are they are heavily medicated and may be hours from being institutionalized.

Someone mailed me a plaque recently. It says:

TEENAGERS! Tired of being harassed by your parents?
Act now. Move out. Get a job and pay your own
bills while you still know everything.

I hung it up in my study.

It went missing the very next day.

Teenagers want to be in charge. I say we let them…just not quite
yet. First, we let the air out of their tires and put sugar cubes in their gas
tanks. Wait—I guess that would be *our* gas tanks. Scratch that idea.

Squinty-Eyed Prophets

It's time to be honest. Contrary to everything I've just written, the
strangest thing happened when our children turned into adolescents: I
discovered that—stay with me here—I absolutely *loved* the teenage
years. You may think I'm crazy (and you may have a point), but I will
not apologize for a second.

Yes, these almost-adults are moody, sometimes obnoxious, and rela-
tionally challenged. Yes, they listen to music that sounds like someone is
throwing lawn darts through a jet engine. True, the teenage years are like
a game of golf: terrible and fabulous and heartbreaking and wonderful,
all in the space of a few hours. But I wouldn't trade these days for anything, not even a peaceful night's sleep.

When our children were young, I squeezed them into a grocery cart
and pushed them around supermarkets seeing if I could find products
that would line up with the coupons I'd clipped. Sometimes I'd try to
swap my cart with other people, but they never accepted my offer.

Older folks would trundle over to us wearing foreboding frowns.
Squinty-eyed, they would peer over their bifocals and offer advice that
went something like this: "You think things are bad *now*. You just wait.

Soon they're gonna wanna date and drive your car." Then they'd shuffle off to the Prune/Bran Flake aisle.

Well, I'd like to tell you that they were wrong. Contrary to the fears and paranoia programmed into us by television and the squinty-eyed prophets of doom, my favorite parenting years so far have been the teenage years. Lest you think I am delusional right now, allow me first to agree with you.

Yes, teenagers are crazy.

The Trouble with Teens

I remember a particularly wild-eyed and frantic woman who said to me, "My teenagers remind me why certain animals eat their young." In Old Testament times they used to stone the odd teenager, which helped keep the others alert and home by 10 p.m. I wonder sometimes if the parents weren't the ones down front with the biggest rocks.

When our children were small we begged them to finish their broccoli. "Come on," we'd cajole, "just one more bite. *Puh-leeze?*"

Now that they are teens, they finish their plate. They finish our plate. They clean out the fridge, the freezer, and the pantry (but not the dishwasher). Then they look at the dog dish and think, *Hey, how bad can that be?*

When our children were small, we used to send them off on their bikes, praying they wouldn't hit a tree. We're still praying, because now they're driving our cars.

My daughter loves to drive. She jangles the keys in front of me like a hypnotist. "Come on, Dad, you are feeling generous. And there are stores open somewhere." If she loves anything more than driving, it's shopping. In fact, Rachael loves shopping so much that she signed up for shop class last year. I kid you not. And when she arrived, she discovered she was the only girl there, surrounded by teenage boys. Not a single one of the boys minded. Nor did she.

When our children were small, we used to pray, "Lord, please help them sleep through the night." Now that they're teenagers, we can't get them to wake up. They are in their prime sleeping years. Jeff recently returned from a week at Bible camp, and he slept a full twenty-three hours in a row, weary from memorizing Scripture. "That's not sleeping," I told Ramona. "That's a coma."

Girls began e-mailing. I told him to give out his new e-mail address: jeff@mysonisnothere.com.

The other day he came through the door and said, "Dad, I'm thinking of getting an earring. Maybe some tattoos."

"That's quite a coincidence," I said, slowly hiking the cuffs of my pants. "I was thinking of having all my pants hemmed just below the knees. And getting a T-shirt that says, 'I'm Jeff Callaway's dad.' "

He laughed so hard he forgot about the earring.

Somewhere within this illustration lies the key to retaining your sanity during the Middle Ages. Five keys, actually. But before we get to them, let me explain that I suffer from ADD and have always written short chapters. So feel free to set the book down and put on a pot of coffee before you turn the page.

Or you may want to find a teenager to read the list at the beginning of this chapter aloud to you. Just remember to take your heart medication first.

You have two choices for dinner tonight. Take it or leave it.

5

I Used to Have Money, Now I Have Teens

If you want to recapture your youth,
just cut off his allowance.

AL BERNSTEIN

People ask if I really have ADD, and I say, "Sorry, could you repeat that? I got distracted." The truth is, I've always had trouble paying attention. Except when our children's friends come over. I pay very close attention when they take to looting and pillaging our pantry like locusts. "Hey!" I ask, "What do you think this is? A buffet?"

They smile and laugh and help themselves to more cereal.

That's the trouble with making a living as a funny guy. They think I'm kidding.

I smelled something out of the ordinary one night about 11:30 p.m., slipped on my housecoat, and found a neighbor boy in our kitchen frying up a steak I had paid good money for. My son had fallen asleep on the sofa. I asked the neighbor boy if he wanted my wallet, seeing as we were out of potatoes and he might need some. He said, "Sure." Expecting a teenager to limit himself to six meals a day is as naive as listening for something original in an echo.

But all in all, it's not so bad. The squinty-eyed prophets in the grocery store programmed me to believe that the worst is yet to come. That amid the rebellion and horror of the teen years, I will lose my sense of humor, my dignity, my wallet, and my hair. They were wrong about the first two. Oh sure, we've had our moments of fear and uncertainty. We've shed some tears, bought some Tylenol, and lost some sleep.

But five keys keep us thriving in a period of life when so many are just surviving. I'll lay them out over the next two chapters, using the acronym TEENS to tell you what they are.

1. Try Laughter

Everyday life can be deadly serious for a teenager. Take, for instance, the following scenario:

Monday. A gorgeous girl named Madison winks at you, and your heart goes *ka-blam!* She says she is thinking of marriage, but you may not be ready for such a commitment. Not before Saturday.

Tuesday. You realize that Madison was really winking at your best friend, and you want to plunge off a cliff in despair.

Wednesday. You score a touchdown in front of a thousand screaming peers! Madison is there! Too bad you were running the wrong way!

Thursday. You start talking to Olivia—the girl who was standing behind Madison when she winked at your best friend—and after a deep conversation that lasts six or seven minutes, things appear to be getting serious. So serious she wants you as a friend on Facebook, and you decide to buy a ring on eBay.

Friday. Your mother tells you that Olivia is your first cousin, and your best friend asks you to be his best man when he marries Madison tomorrow. Your only consolation is that he agrees to buy the ring you purchased on eBay.

The American novelist Jessamyn West once wrote, "At fourteen you don't need sickness or death for tragedy." She was right. It's surprising that teens pay good money to ride roller coasters; they're already on one. They can move from elation to depression in the space of about four seconds. Each zit is leprosy. Each magazine cover mocks them with what they'll never be. When Rachael was sixteen and had no boyfriend, Valentine's Day was like tin foil on a filling. "It should be renamed SAD—Singles' Awareness Day," she joked.

To complicate things, teenagers wonder whose rules to respect, whose lifestyle to adopt, and who on earth kidnapped their body and began performing experiments on it.

How I thank God for the stability of the home where I grew up, a home where laughter was never far away. I know of few assets more valuable in unpredictable and difficult times than a tantalizing haven where contagious laughter is present. Wholesome laughter is a testimony to our children that everything's gonna be okay, that God is big enough to see us through the next exam, the next relational hiccup, the next bout with acne.

2. Exercise Flexibility

Last summer my wife and I were standing on a beach far from home when someone interrupted our conversation. "Phil? It's Gerry. How you doing?" Though we had grown up a few blocks apart, I hadn't seen Gerry in years. (Note: If you think that's his real name, I have Enron stocks I'd love to sell you.)

Immediately Gerry launched into memories of his hometown, memories you wouldn't want in your scrapbook. He told us how his father had crushed his spirit and his tape collection, verbally stiff-arming his son in almost every conversation while quoting Scripture to defend his actions. His was formula parenting, with control being point number one. Sadly, Gerry hadn't been home in years.

Chuck Swindoll wrote, "When it comes to rearing teenagers, rigidity is lethal. Parents who refuse to flex, who insist on everything remaining exactly as it was in earlier years, can expect their kids to rebel."[7] Wise words, those.

I'm not the sharpest knife in the drawer, but I'm learning that good parents change and adapt and listen more than they lecture. That suppertime and bedtime can be more significant in a child's upbringing than school and sports—or even church.

My wife is a morning person. Our teenagers don't want to go to bed until morning. Thankfully, Ramona has the foresight to know that a sturdy cup of tea will keep her awake long enough to watch them eat us out of house and home.

Flexibility is gold when it comes to investing in teens. Last month our younger son turned our basement into a teenage hangout, complete with a 680-volt drum set, three electric guitar amplifiers with volume controls so small no one can find them, a sofa that was at its best before the 1970s, and a stereo system with surround sound and things called "woofers" and "tweeters." But we're okay. We figure if our kids are gonna party, we'd like it to happen about twenty feet away. The music may be annoying, but we're getting to the age where we can't hear it anyway.

6

Baloney Detectors

The old believe everything; the middle aged suspect everything;
the young know everything.

OSCAR WILDE

f life were fair, we'd be born at about ninety-three and slowly grow
toward our teenage years, where we would have enough money to
really enjoy our good health. But life isn't fair, and the teenage years
move fast—unless you're parenting your way through them. I told
someone recently that I think Sundays are a particularly difficult day for
raising teenagers. Also, Monday morning through Saturday night.

But when hasn't this thing called parenting been difficult? When have
you heard the mother of two toddlers say, "You know, we have such peace
and harmony now. The house is so clean, and I'm feeling overly rested"?

We've covered the T and the first E. Let's look at the last three keys:

3. Encourage Discernment

We taught our children, from the time they were small, with question
marks. We challenged them when they spouted clichés. We asked questions they would be asked in the big bad world, and we did it in a way that
was fun and challenging. To this day, their friends will sit in our living room
a few feet from a dormant television and discuss everything from politics
to alcohol to evolution. I believe there is no safer place to think through

difficult issues than under the guidance of godly parents who love God's Word and think teenagers are the coolest things since Brylcreem.

Never in history has a generation had more bad choices so close by. As parents, we'd find it easier to run than to reason. It would be easier to unplug than teach understanding. But model discernment we must, unless we want them to float through life with the crowd that's heading toward the waterfall.

Teenagers have their baloney detectors set on high. They can smell a fake from clear across the church. They don't expect us to be cool—to know who Tom Cruise's latest wife is, for example. But they do need us to be real. To say we're sorry. To be vulnerable.

When a friend of mine discovered that his son had left curious

Child-Rearing for Dummies

It takes a village to raise a child, claims the old African proverb. But it takes only ten steps to raise the village idiot. Here they are:

1. Avoid laughter at all costs. Raise your eyebrows a lot. Glower, grimace, scowl, and frown. Don't celebrate the good times. Make your home a miserable place to be. Show them that the fruit of the Spirit is dried-up prunes.
2. Spoon-feed them religion. Tell them the answers, don't ask questions. Don't talk about your faith. Hang nothing on your wall to indicate your beliefs. Stick with real nice wall hangings you won from vacuum-cleaner salespeople.
3. Rarely support your spouse in decisions or discipline. Criticize each other in front of the kids. Never let them catch you necking.
4. Watch so much TV that your eyes get square. Make it the central object in your home. Use the TV as a baby-sitter. Place at least one in

footprints on the Internet, he was devastated but not surprised. "I knew enough about my own wicked heart," he told me. "So I sat down with him and talked of the difficulty I've had making the right choices, but how, with God's help, I've taken steps to make them—steps that have likely saved my marriage."

Our teens need to know that we were teenagers once, even if it was back before the invention of electricity.

4. Nurture Through Affirmation

Teenagers aren't too old to hear how wonderful they are or how much they are loved. There are enough voices out there telling them they aren't

each child's bedroom at an early age. Wouldn't want him or her reading books.

5. Buy everything on credit, and lunge at anything that says, "No payments until March."

6. Gossip habitually. Have roast preacher for lunch each Sunday. Stew your boss. Chew on your mother in-law. Talk about other people's problems, but don't admit to any of your own. And whatever you do, don't pray for others.

7. Value your children for what they do, not who they are. Compare your children to their siblings. Comment often on their looks. Fixate on the negative. See all that's wrong with your children and nothing that's right.

8. Show them they are less important than your work, your car, and your golf game. Show them that sports are more important than church attendance.

9. Avoid reading the Bible and praying together. Turn them loose without a road map, road signs, guardrails, or a center line, and supply them with bald tires and faulty brakes, then be surprised when they crash.

10. When tough times come, run.

cool enough, thin enough, tall enough, or rich enough. So affirm them every chance you get.

My teenagers have doubted my sanity at times, but never my love for them. They know there is no hour of the day or night during which they are forbidden to flop on my bed and tell me their problems. I may keep right on sleeping, but at least they can talk. Sure, there are times I'd rather lecture than listen. I'd rather watch *The Amazing Race* than take them out for a greasy basket of fries. But in this kick-you-while-you're-down world, our teens are starving for a pat on the back, a listening ear, and to hear those three magic words: "Hey, waytago! Youdabest!"

I once asked Bill Hybels, teaching pastor of the fifteen-thousand-member Willow Creek Church in suburban Chicago, what he would like his children to say about him when he's gone. He replied, "That I was their biggest cheerleader."

When I leave on a trip without my kids, I sometimes leave them notes pasted to their mirrors or placed atop their pillows. I always sign them with, *Your Biggest Fan—Dad.* They do not greet me at the airport with a hug and a kiss anymore, but I have yet to hear a complaint about one of those notes. In fact, I often find them propped up beside their beds.

Sprinkled throughout the diaries of atheist Madalyn Murray O'Hair were these words: "Please, somebody, somewhere, love me."[8] We are never too old to be told how much we are loved.

5. Stay Connected

Do whatever it takes to keep the lines of communication open. We Callaways are not an extravagant bunch, but through the years we've invested in season passes at the golf course and dropped almost everything at the possibility of a family vacation. After our family returned from traveling across an ocean (thanks to Ol' Uncle Air Miles), someone squinted oddly at me and asked, "You took your kids?" You bet we did. I have yet to meet someone in a nursing home who ever regretted such an investment. Besides, our children talk often of continuing this tradition after they have families of their own. They're in…if I pay.

Those who are wise enough to allow their teens room to breathe, who listen more than lecture, and who remain calm when screaming seems like the better option will find that the teenage years are invigorating, adventuresome, and even—particularly when you least expect it—rewarding.

And for those who are afraid of seeing the teenage years come to an end, don't worry. There isn't a teenager I know who hasn't gone out into the brave new world without eventually returning home starved. And carrying a bundle of dirty laundry.

7

Squeeze the Day

*I took my mother-in-law to Madame Tussaud's
Chamber of Horrors and one of the attendants said,
"Keep her moving, sir, we're stock-taking."*
LES DAWSON

☙

*Men past forty
Get up nights,
Look out at city lights
And wonder
Where they made the wrong turn
And why life is so long.*
ED SISSMAN

I n my thirties I was an unbeliever regarding the Midlife Crisis. In my forties, I flew through various stages in rapid succession: skeptic, agnostic, and the one at which I have now arrived—convert.

Nothing about my childhood prepared me for getting older. For one thing, I thought my schoolteachers would kill me. I was thirteen when I realized my name wasn't Smarten Up. But somehow those frazzled teachers restrained themselves and here I am, waking up each morning gazing into the mirror at a middle-aged balding guy who looks exactly like my dad, and thinking to myself, *You have two options: Shave and keep moving, or break the mirror.*

A friend of mine says you officially enter middle age when your age starts to show around your middle. Another reassuring soul claims it arrives when both your parents and your children start telling you what's best for you.

For some of us, the Middle Ages is an emotional state of anxiety in which we realize that the expiration date on our bodies is rapidly approaching, causing us to reflect on the fact that we have accomplished little since placing third in the eighth grade science fair for our research on firecrackers.

The German word for midlife crisis, *Torschlusspanik,* literally means "the panic of closing doors." (The Russian word is *Vuttzadealwithmyhairscavich.*) Somewhere between the ages of thirty-eight and fifty-three, most of us enter a life stage where our children begin staying up late after tucking us into bed. Who knows what they're doing? They could be writing their names on the back of our expensive knickknacks.

The following questions may help you determine whether or not you are in the midst of such a crisis. Then again, these questions may not help at all. But I hope they'll be good for a smile or two.

The Midlife Quiz

1. When I stand in front of the mirror, I:
   a. Thank God for His awesome handiwork.
   b. Close my eyes and grind my teeth.
   c. Can see my rear end without turning around.
2. My hair is:

    a. A wavy, natural blond.

    b. Hair? Yes, I remember hair.

    c. Like a struggling oil company. Good production, poor distribution.

3. I believe we could solve this global warming thing:

    a. If all of us would just drive Smart Cars with seating capacity for three people who, combined, weigh as much as a Rice Krispy square.

    b. If my kids would just keep the refrigerator door closed.

    c. If we could find a way to harness my hot flashes.

4. When I look at my teenager, I think:

    a. This child is a delight!

    b. Who swapped the baskets in the hospital nursery room?

    c. For this I have stretch marks?

Twenty-Eight Fabulous Facts About Getting Older

(There were more, but we misplaced them.)

1. Life insurance salesmen don't call.

2. You can work up an appetite filling the bird feeder.

3. No more hair on your pillow.

4. All the heartburn makes it easier to diet.

5. You're old enough to die of natural causes.

6. You can't hear your spouse snore.

7. You've finally paid off your college tuition.

8. No more hang-gliding accidents.

9. Your plaid pants are back in style.

10. You get mail every day: bills.

11. No more midlife crisis.

12. You have more bridgework than all of Venice.

13. Tuck in your shirt or leave it out. Who cares?

5. The following statement best describes me:
   a. I am happy in my workplace, content with my body, perky, fresh as a spring morning.
   b. It's a miracle that I'm not out on a ledge somewhere.
   c. I am so confused I dropped my mother off at soccer and my daughter at the gerontologist.
6. When it comes to my job:
   a. I get goose bumps knowing what a blessing I am to have around.
   b. Job? I ended my last one the way I began it—I was fired with enthusiasm.
   c. I didn't have to work until I was four. It's been nonstop since.
7. After a visit to the doctor, I:
   a. Am seeing the benefits of eating well and rising at six each day for my nine-mile jog.

14. You have a new lease on life because the doctor has given you three years to live.
15. Your parents don't tell you what to do anymore.
16. You're off the Army Reserve list.
17. You can withdraw from your IRA without penalty.
18. You'll never go through puberty again.
19. No more high school exams.
20. Others offer to carry your luggage. And you let them.
21. Your skateboarding grandson wants your old tweed jacket because it's cool.
22. You learn new vocabulary words like "macular degeneration."
23. Stay up as late as you want. Sometimes until 8 p.m.
24. Entertain neighbor kids with your false teeth.
25. Dinner at 3 p.m.
26. Senior discounts.
27. The police used to warn you to slow down, now it's the doctor.
28. Your kids don't ask for money. They just want it in the will.

b. Comfort myself knowing that my memory may be going, but at least I can retain water.

c. Begin considering acupuncture. I mean, when was the last time you saw a sick porcupine?

8. When I think of finances, I:

a. Know I am right on track due to wise fiscal planning that started when I was twelve.

b. Am wondering how to reconcile my net income with my gross habits.

c. Know that I have all the money I'll ever need if I die by 2 p.m. today.

9. The following best describes my view of aging:

a. Thanks to antiaging books and natural herbs, I will be in peak physical condition well past a hundred.

b. I don't plan to grow old gracefully. Like Rita Rudner, I plan to "have facelifts until my ears join together."

c. Except for the occasional heart attack, I feel as young as ever.

10. When I see my daughter being picked up by her date, I:

a. Give thanks that she has finally met such a fine gentleman.

b. Wish I had installed razor wire in the front yard.

c. Feel like I'm handing a Rembrandt over to a chimpanzee.

11. My favorite song is now:

a. Johnny Nash: "I Can See Clearly Now."

b. Roberta Flack: "The First Time Ever I Slipped a Disc."

c. B. J. Thomas: "Hair Plugs Keep Fallin' Off My Head."

If you answered "a" even once, please leave the room and don't come back until you apologize to the rest of us and are carrying chocolate. If you answered "b" more than twice, please study my book *Laughing Matters*. If you gravitated toward the "c" answers, you qualify for the Midlife Discount. Ask for it at fine restaurants everywhere. Tell them Dr. Phil sent you.

☯

The other day I looked in the mirror and realized once again that I don't have trouble growing hair. But location is a problem. And location is everything when it comes to hair.

I have placed several helpful sayings throughout the house. In my study is an old Ira Wallach quote that says, "Statistics indicate that as a result of overwork, modern executives are dropping like flies on the nation's golf courses."

There's a Bible verse on my fridge: "He must increase, but I must decrease" (John 3:30, KJV).

And now there's the Midlifer's Motto on my mirror: "Therefore we do not lose heart. Though outwardly we are wasting away, yet inwardly we are being renewed day by day" (2 Corinthians 4:16).

I love the word *renewal.* It speaks of better things ahead. It reminds me of a God who has promised to make all things new one day. I began to hang on to that promise a little more tightly as we entered uncharted territory with Mom and Dad.

Sorry, memory upgrades are only available for computers.

8

The Thief

I do wish I could tell you my age but it's impossible.
It keeps changing all the time.

GREER GARSON

For five years my parents lived in the suite we built for them, witnessing the onslaught of our teenagers and raving about their new life. "The best years of our lives," Dad told us over and over again. They loved having teenagers careening around the house. Each morning the sun rose through their living room window. And each morning Dad was greeted by our Maltese dog. The two were inseparable. Dad fed the pooch bananas for breakfast; she would take them from no one else.

Then came the first signs that my father's forgetter was working overtime. Mom found the ice cream under the sink one day, and when she asked Dad how it got there, he joked: "Oh, it was too hard for my dentures."

His sense of humor was intact, but he often grew disoriented, forgetting what organization he was employed by for twenty years, referring to childhood places as if they were just down the street and asking me to take him there.

One night I found him in his favorite chair, his eyes glazed with tears. "I don't know where I should go," he said. "I have no work."

Mom pulled me aside, almost frantic. "Is there anything we can do?" After several visits to the doctor, Dad was diagnosed with early Alzheimer's, that slowly encroaching thief who reduces brilliant scientists to babbling children and saints of God to cursing sailors.

Though he remained kind and gentle, Dad frowned more often, as if he were trying to navigate an unfamiliar car through a strange city, thinking east was north.

I sat with him at night when I could, watching his Toronto Maple Leafs, a struggling hockey team that has offered him mostly misery for years. When we talked of old times, his eyes brightened.

"Remember when you used to cut my hair?"

He smiled.

Dad was no more trained in cutting hair than I am in flying helicopters, but that didn't stop him for a minute. Someone had given him a set of hand-me-down electric clippers, and every once in a while he'd oil them up and take them for a test drive, which is to say that he would sit his sons on a stool, drape an itchy sheet over our bare shoulders, and flip a little switch. The clippers alternated between gentle hum and chain-saw decibel without warning, and if parenting is about making memories, this was parenting extraordinaire.

"Just take a little off the sides," we would beg, knowing full well that Dad had always wanted to be a farmer, and this was as close as he would get to haying season.

"Eh?" Dad would say. "I can't hear you."

After spending a few minutes on one side of my head, he would go around to the other, and—relying solely on memory—try to even things up. I wore a lot of hats back then, dreaming of a time when crew cuts would be back in style.

Dad sat in his rocking chair and grinned as I reminded him of those days. Then he took me by surprise. "It's your turn," he said. "I need a trim."

Few things have given me greater pleasure than this sweet revenge. But as I cut, I thought about the days ahead, and I began to worry. There's an old Jewish saying: "Two things in the world you absolutely should not worry about: what can be fixed and what cannot be fixed. What can be fixed should be fixed at once, without worry. What cannot be fixed, can't be fixed—so why worry about it?"

It sounds good on paper, but I come from a long line of gifted worriers. And so as the days passed, I worried about what to do next. And I asked questions of God, questions I'd never wrestled with before: *How can someone who has spent a lifetime loving and serving You be rewarded this way? What purpose is there in this anguish, in this seeming abandonment? How do I do the right thing given these circumstances? How do I honor my father when honoring him will surely include putting him in the hands of strangers more qualified than I one day soon? And by the way, I have other responsibilities too, Lord. I know I'm not supposed to feel resentment, but it's creeping in.*

One night while running my hands along a shelf filled with books my father had given me, I came across the story of an aged man who lived in his only son's house.

When evening came, the whole family would gather around the big oak dining table to share a meal together. The son and his wife treated the old man well. And he took great pleasure in watching his grandson Matthew grow. He loved to take the child onto his lap and tell him stories.

As the years slid by, the old man's hands began to shake. Sometimes he would spill his tea because of those trembling hands, or he would drop a bowl. And little by little his son became more and more impatient with him.

One evening, as the family sat at the dinner table, the old man accidentally hit his bowl with the soupspoon and the bowl broke in half, spilling soup onto the tablecloth and onto his lap. His son stood to his feet and hissed under his breath, "I'm tired of you spilling food on our good tablecloth and breaking our good dishes! If you can't eat with manners, eat alone."

The next day, the son brought home a wooden bowl. He set a table in the old man's bedroom, using an old sheet as a tablecloth, and served him his food in the wooden bowl.

The old man said nothing and ate his meals alone day after day.

One day when the son came home from work, he noticed Matthew working on something in the corner. "What keeps you so busy today?" he asked.

The boy looked up from his work. "I'm making a bowl, carving it from wood all by myself," he said.

His father was surprised. "A wooden bowl? What will you use it for? We have such beautiful dishes."

The little boy answered, "I'm making this bowl for you. When you grow old like Grandpa, and your hands begin to shake, I'll have this wooden bowl ready to give you in your little room."

The man stood still, staring at the bowl. Then he rushed to his father's room and fell to his knees. "Forgive me, Father. Forgive me for not showing you the respect and honor due you." And he wept.

The father forgave his son. And that evening when the family gathered at the big round table, the old man sat at the place of honor.

I bit my lip hard at the conclusion of the story and pledged before God to honor my dad in this mysterious new chapter of life. And I wondered about my own children. What would they do with me when it's my turn to put popsicles in the dryer?

9

Eight Simple Rules for Dating My Son

I never expected to see the day when girls
would get sunburned in the places they do now.

WILL ROGERS

It's surprising how much you can learn when three teenagers are hanging around the house eying your car keys.

For instance, I learn humility whenever my daughter says, "Why did you get a haircut? Nothing's happening up there."

I learn self-control whenever I can't find the remote control. Or when my son informs me that eighteen friends are coming to watch three movies in fifteen minutes and that they haven't eaten in four days.

I learn about history from one of my sons, whose room looks like Pompeii.

I learn diplomacy when shopping with my daughter, something I have been suckered into only twice. (I would like to tell you I also learn patience while shopping with her, but that is still a ways off.)

I learn that teenagers are too old to do things kids do and too young to act like adults. So they do things no one else would dare.

And I learn that times have changed.

When I was a teenager, boys chased the girls. I remember the day in tenth grade when a blonde named Ramona moved in next door, and I made it my life verse to love my neighbor as myself. I remember how my science, math, and geography grades began to plummet in the wake of her presence, and how I pursued her across the vast ocean of courtship by phone, by foot, and in my father's car.

Back in those primitive years before the invention of helpful objects like cell phones that work underwater, we boys spent a good deal of time chasing girls. We planned for it, we paid for it, and we preened for it. But something happened a few short years ago: role reversal. Girls began chasing boys.

They are aggressive. They are like hungry lionesses preying on limping antelope. They yell out car windows at them. They call them on the telephone. We fathers greet these calls with the same enthusiasm we reserve for telemarketers. "You'd like to speak with my son?" we say. "I am sorry, he is on a mission trip to Zimbabwe where he is marrying several local girls."

The caller does not laugh at this point. In fact, she thinks she has the wrong number, hangs up, and calls again.

This time we try something different: "Is this Emma, Sophia, or Ashley? There are so many, I get you mixed up." Believe me, this one works. Try it for yourself if you doubt me.

Since my sons are both receiving calls from lovely girls who I am sure will make fine wives for someone in twenty or thirty years, I have decided to issue an edict to help them increase their chances of that someone being one of my children. I understand there is a list for daughters, but not for sons. Until now. Though shorter than Martin Luther's Ninety-Five Theses, I believe this list is worth nailing to the front door. I will be doing so myself later today. With a staple gun.

Eight Simple Rules for Dating My Son

1. If you would like to talk with my son, please do this in the church foyer when the lights are on. Remember to bring your family Bible.

2. If you call my house to talk with my son, your call may be monitored by our customer service department.

3. My son is sixteen. The following locations and activities are acceptable for your date. Um…I am drawing a blank here.

4. If you want to hang out with my son, you will have to put up with me. I am out on a weekend pass from a nearby institution and don't have a clue what I will do or say next.

5. My son cannot use my minivan to drive you to a mall. The van is already booked that year.

6. Please do not touch my son. Do not lean up against him unless you are falling over and in danger of injuring yourself or plunging from a cliff. Do not even pull lint from his ear. I have been trying to do this for years, and he will not let me. He can do this himself.

7. I am aware that it is considered fashionable for girls your age to wear Britney Spears T-shirts that do not reach their low-slung pants or necklines that sink lower than the Russian ruble. My wife and I have discussed this, and since we want to be fair and open-minded about it, you are free to show up in such attire. My wife will affix it properly to your body with a glue gun.

8. Above all else, please remember that we've been praying for this boy since before God gave him breath, and we will continue to. If you're the one, we've been praying for you, too.

When and if he chooses a godly girl, we will be happier
than Mr. and Mrs. Turtle when they finally exited Noah's
Ark, but until then we'll keep praying that both of you will
pursue Jesus first, and watch everything else fall into place.

P.S. If you are a teenage girl who has read this and still has a smile
on your face, go ahead and call. Our number is 1-800-321. If you somehow get through, just remember that your call may be monitored by our
customer service department.

Enjoy each moment, Sandra. They grow up so fast.

In Sickness

It is remarkable with what
Christian fortitude and resignation we
can bear the suffering of other folks.

JONATHAN SWIFT

Before our children entered their teen years, Ramona began having seizures—grand mal seizures, they call them. I assure you, there is nothing grand about them. A typical episode saw her muscles seize up and her body slump to the floor in a rigid and seemingly lifeless heap. Then would begin a period of violent convulsions during which I held her and prayed my favorite prayer. These random occurrences lasted up to an hour at a time and frightened the living daylights out of us both. Unable to drive, uncertain how to plan each day, Ramona slid into a dark pit John Bunyan referred to as the Slough of Despond.

One doctor informed us that sleep deprivation and alcohol abuse are two major causes of seizures. Then he stopped talking, his eyes darting from Ramona to me.

"I've thought of alcohol," she admitted.

"She's as dry as my high school teachers' jokes," I interjected. "But sleep deprivation, now—you've heard of Irish twins? We almost had Irish triplets. She hasn't slept since 1986."

The seizures continued to worsen. One night I asked Ramona if there was anything I could do to alleviate some of the pressure around the house. "Hire a maid," she smiled.

"No, really," I repeated. "What can I do?"

"You're going through enough with all of this," she responded. "I'll be fine." Ramona could never be accused of inconveniencing anyone. Lend her an egg; she'll bring you back a full carton.

"When would you like me home?" I asked her.

"Can you find a way to be here for breakfast and get the kids ready for school?"

I told her I would find a way.

A Franciscan Benediction

May God bless you with discomfort
    At easy answers, half-truths, and superficial relationships,
So that you may live deep within your heart.
    May God bless you with anger
At injustice, oppression, and exploitation of people,
    So that you may work for justice, freedom, and peace.
May God bless you with tears
    To shed for those who suffer pain, rejection, hunger, and war,
So that you may reach out your hand to comfort them and
    To turn their pain into joy.
And may God bless you with enough foolishness
    To believe that you can make a difference in the world,
So that you can do what others claim cannot be done
    To bring justice and kindness to all our children and the poor.
Amen

"And how about the rest of the morning, just to massage my feet?"

I told her she was pushing it.

"I just wonder about the kids," she said, her voice trailing away. "How they're handling this."

"I promise you something," I told her. "I'm not much good with massage, and my cooking needs work, but I will always be here for you and for them."

Over the years I've missed a boatload of deadlines. I've hit the wrong net in hockey. I've deposited hundreds of golf balls in fine creeks everywhere. But, thank God, I've never broken that promise.

Sometimes the children and I enjoyed the weirdest concoctions for breakfast. Did you know that you can disguise almost anything in an omelet? I invented porridge à la mode, much to their delight. Sure, they had stomachaches by lunch, but it's a happy kind of stomachache best treated with a large bowl of fresh raspberries topped with maple syrup.

Some of my best memories of those years come from taking the three of them bowling after dinner. Or swimming. Or out for ice cream (as if we needed more). Before bed we curled up on the sofa together, and I read a Bible picture book or told them a story of my childhood. I remain convinced that story hour is one of the greatest bonding opportunities parents are afforded. To leave the TV off and read books is the closest some of us come to pure sainthood.

The stories often gave way to discussions and almost always to laughter. And before I tucked them in, I prayed aloud and blessed them and told them that of all the children in the world, I couldn't have picked out three better ones—and I meant every word.

I have had the pleasure of traveling the world, of attending professional sporting events, of eating and sleeping in the finest hotels, but I assure you that the memory of these pleasures does not bring a smile to my face like the memory of those evenings on the sofa.

A lady with a prunish look once pulled me aside to tell me that seeing their mother have seizures would be hard on children, that I really needed to shield them better. I'm not quite sure what she had in mind—sending them somewhere in a spaceship? (She would really think I'd gone over the edge if she knew that we later invited my parents to live with us.)

Of course I'd love to protect my children from pain, but life happens instead. And as it comes along, so does mercy and—thank God—grace.

I see brief glimpses of that grace in the fact that these three kids still want to hang around us. Okay, not always. But come bedtime most nights, I notice them lingering in the living room like they want me to pronounce the benediction or something. And so, whenever I can, I do. If we have time, I read to them from a rich biography of some great hero of the faith or a quick story I've clipped from somewhere. The time allotted me is shorter now because of their schedules, so sometimes we just sit and talk as they munch on their bedtime meals. Just as we did when they were small, we finish our day with prayer. And I tell them that of all the children in the world, I couldn't have picked out three who eat more.

After months of testing, diagnosis, and the eventual prescription of antiseizure medication, Ramona's health slowly returned. All of us watched with thanksgiving as she gradually emerged from the Slough of Despond.

I do not wish to trivialize the many lessons we learned about suffering and pain and compassion for the struggles of others. In hindsight, I have not experienced growth apart from difficulty; in fact, I doubt I have learned one solitary thing worth remembering that was not forged in the furnace of suffering. But certainly one of the greatest lessons our family has learned is this: When it comes right down to it, the only way to face a crisis that makes any sense at all—is together. And the only direction to face—is up.

11

From Hollywood to Iowa

Electricity will replace God.
The peasants should pray to it; in any case, they will
feel its effects long before they feel any effect from on high.
VLADIMIR LENIN

@@

When I pray, coincidences happen. When I don't, they don't.
ARCHBISHOP WILLIAM TEMPLE

There was a time in my life when I hadn't much use for prayer. "If I should die before I wake" was whispered without much heart in it. After all, I was six. What would I die of? A heart attack? Kidney failure? Hardening of the arteries? Then the day came when my older brother threatened to kill me. And the prayer was whispered with a little more conviction.

This is how it is with life. Our prayers mirror our level of desperation. As we age, more and more is taken out of our hands. As we watch earthly power slip from our grasp, we begin to look for power elsewhere.

I used to wonder how it was that really old and wrinkled people in their forties could pray so much. Now I'm beginning to understand that many of them were experiencing the family squeeze. They had parents and, if they prayed without ceasing, probably teenagers too.

That's the stage at which we find ourselves. Our dear sons, who once grabbed on to our knees and rode around on our feet, are out who-knows-where with gorgeous girls their age who have learned to use lipstick. We wonder why the Bible does not mention Jesus during His teen years. Some believe it's because His parents refused to talk about it.

One of the most profound things I've learned recently is to stop discussing my parenting problems with parents my own age. Parents who have children older than yours have something called perspective, an invaluable asset when you're raising children who used to leave sharp toys on the stairs and are now making life decisions while their hormones rage. Parents of kids the same age as yours seldom admit to you that they stay awake at night worrying and praying and pulling out their hair. But older parents have nothing to lose by being honest. They smile and nod and say things like, "I know. I remember the same thing. It'll be okay. Your hair will grow back. Some of it, at least."

I am bolstered by these people, but mostly at the end of the day when I'm lying in bed and three children are in different cars being steered by boys who not so long ago were driving their tricycles through mud puddles, I pray.

And sometimes, on really good nights, God will spark my ADD into action, and I'll remember stories of answered prayer, stories the most skeptical would at least find amusing.

Simple stories that give me hope.

Back when our kids wanted to travel in the same car as their parents, we journeyed three days to get to Iowa, where I was to address a family camp. I've discovered that the best way for a speaker to gain credibility at family camp is to leave his children at home, but ours have always come along. And I think it's been comforting to other parents to watch them misbehave.

As we sat at dinner the first night, the children munching corn on the cob, the camp director, Earl Taylor, and his wife, Dede, told us a little about the camp. Located on 660 acres of wooded property in central Iowa, Hidden Acres had experienced significant growth the last few years. But with growth came the usual structural hurdles.

Most recently, the camp staff had been praying that God would supply enough money to build a sewer so that frightened campers would not have to hike past bears and wolves and hyenas to use the facilities in the middle of the night.

The staff prayed often.

Nothing happened.

Then one day a semitruck crept up the gravel road, and a gentleman climbed out. "Do you mind if I park my rig here?" he asked, pointing to a hayfield on the southern edge of camp.

Earl, as accommodating a Midwesterner as you'll ever meet, said, "Sure."

Soon the truck driver had another question. "We're filming a little movie, and there are more of us. You know, trailers and some equipment. Oh…and helicopters, too. Is that okay?"

"No problem," said Earl.

The crew was from a little studio out west called Warner Brothers, and they had a few more questions. They were shooting some scenes on a road west of camp. Could they scatter a little straw? Blow it around? "We'll pay you to clean things up," they promised.

Earl said sure.

Next a helicopter landed in the south field, and a bearded man by the name of Steven ducked out of it, along with his personal chef. He was producing a little film about a tornado. The crew called him Mr. Spielberg.

Warner Brothers stayed thirty-six hours on the property filming *Twister*. It took the camp staff three hours to clean up the road. Then they were asked to put all the trash back on the highway; the crew needed to shoot the scene again. Earl said, "No sweat."

Before the trucks and helicopters departed, Earl was handed a check. One that made his mouth drop open and hang there awhile. It was written out for the exact amount they'd been praying for.

A friend rolls his eyes when I mention answered prayer because he is more educated than I and can put a voice to the "hows" of history. How could a God who answers prayer turn a deaf ear while Hitler murdered six million Jews and several million Christians? How could God watch Stalin kill sixty million without doing something? What about Lebanon and Baghdad and Hiroshima?

I don't know quite how to respond. There is so much I don't understand. But late at night I keep circling back to God's obvious leading in my life. I have seen Him give joy when there is no plausible explanation for it. When I'm in the back of an ambulance holding the hand of my unconscious wife while nurses cast sideways glances at each other. And I have sensed the peace of knowing that my children are in His hands, even tonight, no matter who's driving the car.

Earl agrees. Ask him if God answers prayer, and he'll smile and tell you a story. And he'll probably conclude it this way: "When I got that check, I knew what we'd build with it—and we'd do it in memory of Hollywood. They've built their share of sewers. Why not build one in their honor out here in Iowa?"

12

Saint Bernard

Nothing is so contagious as example.

FRANÇOIS DE LA ROCHEFOUCAULD

I've written about hope from time to time, perhaps because I want so desperately to feel it, to have it stop wriggling away from me when I try and pin it to the mat. Hope is your best club in golf, the hope that on the next shot this stupid little white thing will do what you ask it to, that maybe a miracle will occur and you'll be there to see it.

You need hope in golf; you need it even more when you have three teenagers. Lately I've been praying that these kids will stop grumbling and yelling at each other. That we're not raising complete pagans here. That they will encounter godly people who are full of hope. After all, most of us would rather see a sermon than hear one any day.

My prayers have been especially earnest when it comes to our younger son, partly because he reminds me of myself at his age—filled with mischief and always about three seconds from a very bad decision.

Jeff is a big, tough, stylish kid, handsome and strong, the teenager all the little kids love and the kind girls phone to discuss math problems with (or at least that's what they tell you when they finally get past your customer service department). His laugh was enough to bring the house down when he was a kid, but that contagious laugh began to vanish by the time the boy was twelve and was completely extinct when he turned thirteen. It's a horrible thing to watch someone view life wearing the glasses of a teenager, trading in joy because it isn't so cool.

Our kids have always laughed a lot, partly because they get their sense of humor from my wife's side of the family, whose motto is this: "It's all funny until someone gets hurt. Then it's hilarious!"

I slip on an icy sidewalk, landing on my rear, and these kids will snort and laugh until they hyperventilate. I raise a window to get some air in the room and it slips, landing on my fingers, and they fall off their chairs laughing. But by the time they are teenagers the hyperventilating has pretty much been cured. Life is as serious as a cracked rib. If childhood is spring training, the teen years are extra innings in the World Series. Laughter seems out of place, like a puppy at church.

And so I worried about Jeff's dislocated funny bone, because laughter is surely one of God's purest gifts to us. How I longed to hear that laugh again. The only time it seemed to eke through was during a movie I wouldn't necessarily recommend or when I hit my elbow on the back of a chair. I even wrote the word on a prayer list I keep for each of my kids—*laugh*—believing that God cares about these things as surely as He cares for the other requests on the list: respect, soft heart, attitude, that my son will find a godly wife in about ten years.

To complicate things, the boy was struggling in school. He was late on assignments as often as United Airlines. A teacher called to tell me this and to hint that if he could issue marks below zero, he would give them to my son. Imagine telling your friends you have a minus twenty-three in Chemistry. Not an F, but an H.

My prayers turned more urgent. At night I closed my eyes in the dark and tried to pray, but the whole thing seemed so hopeless that I would get up and turn on CNN. There I found a strange relief knowing that things were at least as awful as I thought. Maybe worse. That the sky really was falling, that situations were bad everywhere, that the good guys were in the minority. Sometimes, if things grew really desperate or I couldn't find the remote, I would open my Bible.

I received a welcome phone call in the midst of all this. It was Compassion, the international child-development agency, asking us to go to the Dominican Republic on a short mission trip. I prayed about it for one-third of a nanosecond, then eagerly said yes. I would run away from home. And take Jeff along.

The teacher caught wind of our escape plans and called to accuse me of taking leave of whatever senses I had left. I thought of something I'd read about the Cuban Missile Crisis, how the Kremlin sent two messages to President Kennedy. One was hostile, the other calm. Kennedy said, "Let's respond to the saner message," and as a result, those elementary school drills where we cowered under our desks in panic were all in vain. So I listened for the saner message. The teacher said I was neglecting what's truly important by taking Jeff out of school, that he should be at home with his teenage skull buried in serious books.

I considered telling this teacher that I learned about 6 percent of what I now know in the classroom, but thankfully I went with a saner response. I am a Christian, and sometimes I am relieved to find myself acting like it. "I'm so glad you care about him," I said, "but I'm really concerned about his spiritual health." I did not say, "I don't want his schooling to interfere with his education." I'm thankful I didn't.

That night I waved the plane ticket in front of Jeff like a carrot. I told him that he'd better smarten up, listen up, and catch up on his assignments, or I would give the ticket to a complete stranger, maybe even the next girl who called. He smiled ever so slightly. "Do your assignments," I told him. The smile was still there when he promised he would.

We were met at the airport in the Dominican Republic by Pastor

Bernard, who has a glow about him like he works at a nuclear power plant. Bernard doesn't say a lot, which is one of the first signs of saint-hood. Mostly he grins, like he knows something you don't. People ask him why he's grinning, and he tells them, "Peace. Joy. Hope." And they want to know more.

Bernard speaks three languages fluently, but he'd rather listen to you. Jeff latched on to him during those ten days. He listened to Bernard's stories of God at work. He watched Bernard tell others of Jesus. And better yet, he saw God for himself—through Saint Bernard.

We stood in a village devastated by a hurricane, but Bernard's face was beaming. "They want me to tell you that their houses are gone but it's okay. The church is still standing." The crowd smiled and nodded. Jeff kicked at a rock and shook his head. We saw children who subsist on food they've scrounged from the dump, kids with hollow eyes and bloated bellies. We helped feed them and saw what child sponsorship can accomplish. When we said good-bye, it was amid tears and ample hugs. Jeff hugged Bernard.

"I'll miss you," said Bernard.

"Me too," said Jeff.

If you were to ask me about my happiest moment of fatherhood, I might mention the night soon after we returned. Jeff's marks were up a little, hovering near the passing mark. I hadn't heard him fight with his sister or grumble about a thing. Not yet. And the laughter was back—not the hyperventilating kind, but his vital signs were good. He was making himself a snack in the kitchen along about mid-night, and I could smell it from our bedroom, so I crept out to see if he would share.

The boy had cracked half a dozen eggs into a bowl, along with a pound of shredded cheese, and thrown an entire package of Canadian bacon into a sizzling frying pan. As he stirred the eggs and cheese together, he said to me, "Dad, I'd like to sponsor a kid in the DR. It's thirty-five bucks a month, right?"

I tried not to let him see my tears, then decided it didn't matter. I'd just watched my son go from talking about Christianity to doing it. From following those who follow Jesus, to following Jesus for himself.

I guess hope always catches us a little by surprise.

Don't be in any rush to grow up, kiddo. I just found out that when you get to be my age, they don't give treats for going to the bathroom anymore.

13

One Ring

*Dear Lord, never let me
be afraid to pray for the impossible.*

DOROTHY SHELLENBERGER

T he earth is divided into two groups of people: those who like *The Lord of the Rings* and those who don't. Ask my eldest child which book of earth is his favorite, and he won't skip a beat. Ask him about a moment when his prayers seemed silly, and he just might smile broadly.

Without a doubt, Steve's favorite book is a story of hobbits and Bilbo Baggins. All 23,000 pages of it. To my utter amazement, he had read all three books in the Rings trilogy by the age of ten. Before we celebrated his fifteenth birthday he had read them thrice and was gearing up for a fourth voyage. *Crazy,* I thought. He should be cleaning my car. He read them between playing basketball and ice hockey and table tennis. He read them in the evenings when he should have been studying. He read them late at night when he should have been snoring. The day I informed him that Peter Jackson was bringing the stories to life on the silver screen, he ricocheted around the living room, pumping his fists.

The filmmakers should have used my son as a consultant. From beginning to end, he can tell you more than you want to know about

Middle Earth, about hobbits and goblins, about the "one ring to rule them all."

Shortly after we attended the first movie together, Steve turned sixteen. This is an age when fathers and sons have whispered conversations about life and love and being all grown up. One night during one of those discussions, I spoke to him about the importance of reaching this milestone of manhood. How, like his favorite hobbit Frodo, he would be faced with great temptations and great opportunities as he journeyed through the darkness of this earth. I said I would like to present him with a small gift as a covenant between him and me that he would walk the way Frodo had walked, choosing to do the right thing, though it cost him everything. I talked of putting God first. Of faith. Of purity. He nodded his approval.

"What's the gift?" he asked. When I told him, he smiled.

The next day I ordered the first item I've ever ordered on the Internet. Scary thing for me. Even scarier price.

On the evening the package arrived, we convened for a family ceremony. The children leaned in, wide-eyed, as I opened a small box. "Hey! It's a Callaway golf ball! Just kidding," I said, then pulled out a wooden box. Inside was a genuine replica of "the one ring." White gold, complete with Elvish engravings.

"What about ours?" whined the other two.

"You wait," I told them.

I read a short verse of Scripture: " 'So fear the LORD and serve him wholeheartedly,' Joshua 24:14. For sixteen years that's been our prayer for you, Steve. That you would honor God and serve Him."

We prayed together, committing this child and his future to God. Then I took the ring, hung it from a gold chain, placed it about his neck, and kissed his forehead before he squirmed away.

There the ring stayed.

Until the night Steve arrived home from school carrying small pieces of the chain. He could scarcely bring himself to tell me.

It had broken, he knew not when.

The ring was gone, we knew not where.

We searched everywhere. Along sidewalks and hallways. Through classrooms and cars. Then we began looking in ridiculous places, like the toolshed and heating vents. Nothing. It was permanently gone, I knew. Hanging about someone else's neck. Adorning another's jewelry case.

So Steve began to pray.

His younger sister and brother joined him too. At suppertime, they prayed that we would find the ring. At breakfast they prayed, believing. I hated to doubt, but I am a grownup. I've gotten very good at it.

"There's more chance of the Chicago Cubs winning the World Series," I told my wife.

"They're not even in it," she said.

"Precisely."

We had other things to pray about too, of course. Things that seemed just as impossible. Decisions related to Mom and Dad and life and work.

Steve told his grandparents about the ring. They didn't know what a Frodo was, but they too began to pray.

Months passed. Winter came and went. The dazzling white snow that covered the field through which my son sometimes walks to school began to melt. And one evening as we sat down to eat together, I noticed a particularly broad grin on Steve's face. As we ransacked a roast chicken, he told us he'd been walking home from school when a glint of reflected sunlight caught his eye. He then held his hand out and opened it.

I couldn't believe my eyes. The ring. White gold, with Elvish etchings. As good as new. Back from Middle Earth.

Oh me of little faith.

Do you know what my prayer had been all this time? That he wouldn't be too disappointed when his prayers weren't answered. Here I was, praying that God wouldn't dash the boy's hopes too badly. There he was, asking God to do the impossible, something He has delighted in doing since the dawn of time.

The ring hangs about Steve's neck from a sturdier chain now. I hope it will serve as a constant reminder to honor the Lord and serve Him wholeheartedly. I hope it will remind the rest of us that those who seek find, that those who ask receive, and that grownups of little faith sometimes get another chance.

14

A Few Good Words

*Accept the fact that there will be moments when
your children will hate you. This is normal and natural.
But how a child handles hate may determine whether
he will go to Harvard or San Quentin.*

ANN LANDERS

ଚ⍥

Abounding grace is the hope of mankind.

A. W. TOZER

H ave you ever wondered if there's hope for the next generation?
I certainly have. They've got more earrings than brain cells.
They're confused. They don't know which way to point their
hats or how high to pull their pants. They have problems with
their eyesight. They can't find a thing to eat in a fridge full of food nor a
thing to wear in a closet full of clothes. They're glued to their cell phones—
when they're not chatting online in brief, meaningless sentences.

Whenever I share such thoughts with my wife, she just grins. I
worry about the kids, she tells me, because they're a lot like me. And she
is right. Not a lot of grownups lit up with hope when they saw me.

Author's note: Names have been changed in this chapter because these guys are still bigger
than I.

I was a skinny child. So skinny that I had only one vertical stripe on my pajamas. So skinny that I needed suspenders to hold up my Speedo. So skinny that I was swimming in a lake one summer and a dog came out to fetch me—three times. My mother used to scrub laundry on my rib cage. People looking for a toothpick at the dinner table would grab me. You get the picture.

I wasn't a particularly bad-looking child—my father did not spank my mother when I was born, as my older brother claimed—but I was uncommonly thin, and it took me years to discover any humor in it. I remember as if it were an hour ago the time a beautiful girl in our school rode past me on her silver bicycle and shouted, "Hi, Skinny!" as if that were my given name. I would rather she had leveled a potato gun at me and pulled the trigger.

I suppose I became a writer partly as a response to the enormous humiliation of being teased as a child. A sense of humor and my ability with words were the only weapons in my arsenal. So I kept my wit sharp and my tongue forked.

In elementary school a classmate broke my thumb with a hockey stick, threw snow in my face, then laughed as I cried. His name was Ken, but I called him other things, things I'm not proud of. I told him things of which he had no idea. Things involving his family history and his future.

I knew he was going to break my other thumb. Instead he quickly skated away. I realized something wonderful that day: sticks and stones can break bones, but words can shatter something far deeper.

In high school, an upperclassman named Larry approached me in the hallway and said, "Callaway, you're so skinny, we should slide you under the door when we need stuff."

I couldn't think of a gracious response, so I said, "Well, you're so fat, you broke your family tree!" He was stunned.

I was on a terrible roll. I said, "You're so fat, when you bend over, you cause an eclipse on three continents." I couldn't stop myself now. I had thrown my tongue into gear before engaging my brain. "You're so fat, you beep when you back up."

I thought he would murder me and the jury would unanimously acquit him. Instead, the color drained from his face as he turned and walked away.

That same year I discovered writing. I was about ninety pounds at the time, which was just enough to make the keys on the typewriter go down. My first critical review came from classmates in response to my essay, "A Day in the Life of an English Student," in which I pointed out various physical characteristics of our teacher and just how boring it was to be in his class. I believe his reason for reading my essay publicly was to humiliate me. To show the class that using his name in an assignment was improper and unwise. That ridiculing his teaching habits would not go unpunished.

It backfired big time. The students clapped. They cheered. They loved me. A few rose to their feet. One saluted me.

The teacher stopped reading and wrote across my essay in red ink, "Composition poor. Grammar bad. See me after school." He gave me a D.

As I sat at my desk that afternoon, I began to dream. I dreamed of becoming a writer. Of penning hugely successful novels jammed with humor, sarcasm, and revenge. I dreamed of the day Ken and Larry would want me as their friend, would beg forgiveness for not treating me better.

Two things stood in the way: A mother who prayed for me every day of my life. And a father who promised me a watch if I read one chapter of Proverbs each day for a month.[9] I began to encounter verses like "Reckless words pierce like a sword" (12:18) and "The tongue that brings healing is a tree of life" (15:4).

I remember reading once that the singer Karen Carpenter's fatal obsession with weight control began when she read a *Billboard* reviewer's comment in which he dubbed her "Richard's chubby sister." At the age of thirty-two, Karen died of heart failure.

The tongue can be an ambassador of the heart. Or a deadly weapon.

Somehow the Spirit of God took hold of me. I realized the devastating power of reckless words. And I began to pray that God would transform my tongue and use my words to bring healing and hope.

I believe it is one of the prayers God loves to hear and that He answers it for all of us. I have seen Him do so in the most surprising ways.

I was speaking about God's grace at a large convention recently, and when I stepped off the stage, guess who was waiting for me? Ken. I kid you not. He gave me a bear hug that made my kidneys hurt. There were tears streaming down his face. Ten minutes later, guess who elbowed his way through the crowd? Larry. There were tears in his eyes. Mine too. Two bullies and a skinny kid. On even ground at the foot of the cross. Amazed by grace.

As parents we do what we can, but we always fall short. And God's grace comes in. Surprising each new generation, captivating us, meeting us where we are but never leaving us where it finds us.

"Isn't God good?" said Ken, taking my right hand and squeezing it a little too hard. "How's the thumb?"

"Never better," I said. "Never better."

15 Middle-Age Memories

Dogs lead a nice life.
You never see a dog with a wristwatch.

GEORGE CARLIN

It's a funny thing, this getting older. Okay, maybe not so funny. But interesting. It's an adventure unlike anything we've experienced before. For one thing, our bodies aren't what they used to be. We have to stretch before playing checkers now. We get winded looking at staircases. To make matters worse, those same bodies have simply stopped taking directions. In fact, they've gone on strike. "Feed me," they whimper, "and I will think of serving you again. Feed me large hampers full of cholesterol-stuffed ham and red meat."

Since the age of three I have played ice hockey. But lately when I play, my mind screams at me, saying, "Go get the puck, you fool! It's right there in front of you!" Meanwhile, my body hollers, "I bet Ed's Diner will be open after the game. They serve those nachos with that cheese-flavored lard! Besides, there is a younger guy who wants the puck worse than me. Let him have it!" And my mind, which doesn't hear so well anymore, repeats the words, "Let him have it"—and my body, which rarely follows directions, finally decides to. So I shish-kebab the younger guy with my hockey stick.

The forgetfulness problem is an interesting one too. Recently, at a large gathering, I introduced myself to the same person twice within the space of three minutes.

"But we just met," he said, this younger guy with a razor-sharp mind.

"Aha," I replied, "I was testing you."

Perhaps you've done something similar. You meet someone you haven't seen since high school and want to introduce him to your spouse. You say, "Honey, this is, um…a dear friend of mine from…uh…high school. We were in, uh…a class together. I sat next to him three years in a row… Yes, we were best friends… He was best man at our wedding…and, uh… Do either of you need more punch?"

There are three things we need to remember when it comes to forgetfulness:

1. Our minds are like sponges, but they also leak.
2. The part that doesn't leak isn't of much use.

As early as ninth grade, our brains begin to accumulate junk—years and years of completely useless information—which includes jokes told during recess and the lyrics to seventies songs. Almost every day people ask me important questions about history, about the Christian life—sometimes on radio or national television—and though I am trying to access file folders stored in my brain since youth, all I can think of is a lyric swirling round and round, a lyric I am not making up:

Drop kick me, Jesus, through the goalposts of life…
Straight through the heart of them righteous uprights.

Country songs are to blame for the mass migration of most of my thoughts at vital moments. I cannot count the times I have racked my brain for an important nugget of information, such as where a particular Bible verse is found, where I parked my car, or whether I brought my wife with me to the mall, only to find lurking there a song I first heard in the eighth grade, something like "Folsom Prison Blues" or anything by Tammy Wynette. Just this morning I woke up to discover that "Counting Flowers on the Wall" by the Statler Brothers was going round and round as I shaved. I had not thought of the song for at least twenty-four years.

> Smoking cigarettes and watching Captain Kangaroo
> Now don't tell me, I've nothing to do.

Perfectly good brain cells were wasted on these things, and if I could go back to high school (and there are teachers who insist I should), I would keep the radio off and study more important things, like how to remember the guy's name who sat beside me those three years in a row.

They say that fifty is the new forty, that thanks to modern science and medicine and things like liposuction, we are taking much longer to look our age now. And they are probably right. This chart, however, which is based on a study I considered conducting, shows that the decades are distinctly dissimilar (a completely useless and redundant word I learned in high school and can't forget):

In your forties	In your fifties	In your sixties
You have *The Eagles Greatest Hits* on cassette, LP record, eight-track, CD, MP3, your laptop, and your iPod.	You can remember the advent of the Sharp all-transistor desktop calculator, which weighed in at fifty-five pounds and cost $2,500.	You tell your grandchildren you saw Beethoven in concert and have his autograph but can't remember where it is.
Hair turns gray.	Hair goes underground and starts coming out your nose.	Hair? I had hair?
You can remember where you were when you heard that Elvis Presley died (I was roofing a house with black shingles).	You can remember and hum at least three Elvis songs and have several on gramophone records.	Pelvis? Yes, sit down and I'll tell you what happened the first time I broke my pelvis.

In your forties	In your fifties	In your sixties
You crack jokes about older people and doctors and rubber gloves.	Rubber glove jokes aren't funny to you now. You wince at the sound of snapping rubber.	You try to remember doctors' appointments and jokes about doctors and rubber gloves.
You stand tall for your daughter's wedding.	You keep a chart to measure the height of your daughter's children whenever they visit.	You shrink half an inch and add a little weight.
Your eyesight is pretty good, though you are beginning to hold restaurant menus with your feet.	You can't tell the difference between 60 mph and 80 mph road signs, but the police officer won't believe you.	You remind the officer of his grandparents, and he lets you go.
You see a girl across the room, but for the life of you cannot remember her name.	You ask someone nearby, "What's her name?"	The girl turns out to be your spouse.

Some consider another birthday to be a *millstone*. I consider it a *milestone*, a reminder of the fact that we are one year closer to Home.

Perhaps one of the greatest benefits of reaching middle age is that I can look back through the years with a little wisdom. When I do, I realize that I seldom remember what I was told, but I seldom forget what I experienced. And what I have experienced is this: Through all of the bends and the twists of life, God has not abandoned me for a single solitary second. All I have seen through the years teaches me to believe Him for all I have not seen. It's something I hope you and I never forget.

And I hope you are still sharp enough to notice that I had no third point about forgetfulness.

We made some adjustments since your last visit.

16

About Time

Midlife crisis is that time when you realize that
your children and your clothes are about the same age.
BILL TAMMEUS

೦ა

The years run too short and the days too fast.
The things you lean on are things that don't last.
AL STEWART, "TIME PASSAGES"

The thing about reaching middle age is that if you have any brains left at all, you start to realize you're running out of time. Time to do things you vowed you'd do back when you were twenty-four. And so, one Saturday, you find yourself behind a sixteen thousand–horsepower ski boat being steered by a former high school friend named Attila, hanging on to a towrope, trying to avoid fishing boats and beads of water that smack you in the eyes like buckshot.

"What in the world am I doing?" you're screaming, and Attila thinks you want him to speed up.

Every few weeks I get together with five other middle-aged guys for something we call the Circle of Six. It's an eating group, really, though we founded it with grander plans. The group has been growing (pun intended) for a dozen years now, thanks to some incredible cheesecake of our own making, and as we hit the middle years, I noticed that some of us are engaging in activities we wouldn't have dreamed of back when we still had our minds.

For instance, one of the guys (I won't name names, but I will tell you that Ron Nickel receives this guy's credit card statements) bought a high-powered motorcycle, then sold it when he came within a whisker of crashing. Another took up hang gliding and limped to our meeting a few weeks ago, holding his lower back and making sounds somewhat akin to those of an overworked mule. (Again, I wouldn't dream of telling you his name, but for the sake of this book, we'll call him Vance Neudorf.)

We got to sitting around the fire, the six of us, talking of things we intended to do when we were younger but haven't because we've been held back by time. Or our loving wives. Or our insurance agents.

"I'd like to cycle across the country," said one of us. Everyone nodded.

"Garden with my wife," said another. Everyone gasped.

One even confessed that he'd like to learn the ukulele and give concerts. I won't tell you who it was, but everyone laughed.

Then came stories of parents who had grand plans for an adventuresome retirement, who salted away money for travel only to discover that they'd run out of health once they got there; they'd run out of time.

As I watch my parents age in the suite next door, I am reminded of time's rapid passage. I guess we spend our early years wishing time would hurry up, our middle years trying to find more of it, and our latter years wondering where in the world it went. We get so busy with the blur of schedules and the stuff of earth that we neglect the celebration of today.

Time is one versatile guy. He flies. He heals all wounds. Time can be wasted. Time will tell. Time marches on. Time runs out. Everywhere in the Western world are reminders of time. We have clocks on our wrists and our cell phones, our stereos and dashboards, our street signs and buildings. We dangle clocks around our necks, in our pockets, and in every room of the house. One day archaeologists will dig up our stuff and say, "Hey, they must have worshiped these things. Stand back, this one's still ticking."

I'm told that the average seventy-year-old has spent twenty years working and twenty-three years sound asleep. He has spent seven years eating and drinking, six years in a car, four years sick, two years dressing himself, and about twenty-nine days slathering on mosquito repellent.

Some people are very organized when it comes to time. They write down lists of things they will do with their day. That way, they don't have to spend time remembering things; they can spend their time looking for the paper they wrote the list on.

To avoid the avalanche of time, middle-agers:

- buy juicers
- yogacize
- nip
- tuck
- wear spandex
- medicate
- diet
- visit 4.5 million "antiaging" Web sites
- try another diet, one that "really works"

During midlife, we are constantly trying to make up for lost time. We rush about as if we're going to find it somewhere, hoping all the while that time is on our side. We get so stressed out we start drinking Maalox like it's gravy. We wonder, *What would it be like to slow down? And if we slow down, will we have a nervous breakdown?* Materialism and speed have doused the fire in our souls, and it's time we went looking for matches.

"Teach us to number our days aright, that we may gain a heart of wisdom," wrote the psalmist in Psalm 90:12. And if we number them, we just may find that we don't have enough time left for petty stuff like discussing someone else's failures. Or how the soloist should have tuned up before singing last Sunday. We won't have time to whine and complain that the previous generation got it wrong and the next generation doesn't get it at all. We won't have time for things that are really ugly and disgusting, including much of what's on tabloids and television. We won't have time to sit around comparing what can't be taken to the next world. Things like bank accounts, titles, and achievements.

If we find those matches and reignite that fire in our souls, we will discover that time is precious—that we should spend it brightening someone's day, helping those less privileged, and loving those who are forgotten. After all, no matter our age, we have less time than we think. Yesterday is a memory, tomorrow is an assumption, and this moment that we say we have…just passed.

A wise friend says, "How you spend your time is more important than how you spend your money. Make a mistake with money and it can be fixed, but time is gone." In her excellent book *Time Peace,* my friend Ellen Vaughn reminds us that "in the end, people's beliefs—their worldview—determine their attitude toward time."

As a Christian, I believe we are stewards of whatever God gives us, including the days we have left. Because of Christ we are promised the riches of eternity where time will be extinct, but for now we are allowed the riches of today. I'd like to spend my remaining days spreading grace and joy around. As A. W. Tozer wrote, "May the knowledge of Thy eternity not be wasted on me!"

Who knows? I might even sign up for those ukulele lessons after all.

17

The Twenty-Five-Year Itch

Women now have choices. They can be married,
not married, have a job, not have a job, be married
with children, unmarried with children. Men have the
same choice we've always had: work, or prison.

TIM ALLEN

Love at first sight is easy to understand.
It's when two people have been looking at each
other for years that it becomes a miracle.

SAM LEVENSON

I believe it was the great American theologian Mark Twain who said, "No man or woman really knows what perfect love is until they have been married a quarter of a century." Mr. Twain may have been onto something there, because the truth is, getting through the Middle Ages happily married doesn't seem to be getting any easier. The *Daily Mail* reports that "the fastest-growing age group embarking on divorce proceedings is currently the over-fifties."[10] They call it late-life divorce. One couple said: "People change and we forgot to tell each other." I suppose most couples would admit that they have grounds for divorce. Here are a few stories of how we continue to find grounds for a great marriage.

∽

When Rachael was a three-and-a-half-foot five-year-old with an attitude, she summoned me to her bedroom one night: "Daddy…Haaaalp!"

I found her sitting on the edge of her bed twirling her little green bear and frowning deeply as though I had put cornflakes in her pillow. (Of course, I had not done this. I would do this about five years later.)

"What is it?" I asked.

Lowering the bear, she lifted her head, put her hands on her hips and glared at me. "Are you and Mama gonna get a divorce?" she demanded.

I gulped twice. "Why, honey?"

"I heard you fighting."

I gulped a third time. "But I love Mama. I, uh—"

"Patty's mama said the same thing. Now she's gettin' a divorce." It was like she'd picked up a gavel and was about to sentence me.

"No, Your Honor," I said. "I married Mom for life. Sometimes we don't agree, but that can be a good thing, don't you think?"

She wasn't buying it. "You be nice to her," she scolded.

"I promise I will," I said, leaning over and hugging her tightly. "Did you know that seven years before you came along I stood in a great big church and made a promise?"

"Did you look handsome?"

"I had a mustache."

"Oh."

"I promised God and about three hundred people that I would be your mama's sweetheart all my life. And I'd stand up tomorrow and say the same thing."

"Church is tomorrow," she said as I tucked her and her bear into bed. "You can do it then."

I once thought that if we could just get our marriage launched and through the land mines of the toddler years, we could put it in neutral and coast all the way home. Bring on middle age. It would be a walk in the park.

But now Ramona and I find ourselves married a quarter of a century, a little tired, sitting at the dinner table talking about the kids and finishing sentences for each other.

Me: So I was gonna—

She: But we don't need lettuce—

Me: All right, then I'll—

She: Good, because I was hoping—

Me: Don't worry. I wouldn't—

She: But last time you—

Me: I know. But I promise I won't forget—

She: Chocolate.

Me: Dark chocolate.

Back in 1999, www.over50s.com launched an online dating service. It now boasts more than 250,000 registered users, many of them guys who woke up one Saturday and stood before the mirror, thinking out loud:

"I have been teaching school to eighth graders for twenty-six years, and if I see even *one* more eighth grader this weekend, I am going to go stark raving mad and crash my grocery cart into the watermelons. What was I thinking when I was twenty-two? I didn't even like eighth grade, for Pete's sake. I don't even know who Pete is. I wanna be a… um…a mechanic. Yes, I love cars. In fact, I think I'll go buy a little red convertible right now. I think I'll put on some extra cologne. Buy an iPod. Maybe a Speedo. Do Speedos come in size fifty-two? I'll bet they do. The sky's the limit for me. There's nothing I can't do. I am so excited. Ouch! I think I pulled some fat."

I personally have had trouble completely embracing the midlife crisis, although I will admit that I do drive a really hot-looking silver Pontiac Sunfire. But when I see guys my age with women half their age, I get to wondering, what am I doing watching another Clint Eastwood movie? And when I see them in real life, I wonder what they talk about when they sit around the dinner table and the swagger has become a shuffle.

Him: Hey, do you remember back when…oh, never mind.

Her: Did you hear that Britney and Paris had their hair done the same way the same week?

Him: No, but I was reading—

Her: Like in a book?

Him: Yeah. A book about Vladimir Lenin—

Her: I never really liked the Beatles. But I was like thinking that, like, I might wanna go and like get my nails done and, like, finish looking at the pictures in *Us* magazine.

Him: I was thinking I might want to call my kids.

Her: But they won't, like, talk to you anymore. Remember?

Him: I was thinking that I'm gonna be sick.

Sadly, I meet so many who have discarded a marriage thinking something lustrous was waiting, only to find out it wasn't what they thought—like a greyhound that finally catches a mechanical rabbit.

In church recently we were singing "It's All About You." I heard a shrill little girl's voice behind me. She had changed the words ever so slightly to reflect what many of us sing with our lives: "It's All About *Me*."

A hospital chaplain told me of the lonely, alienated people he tries to comfort. Folks who at some point started singing the song that way.

One recently abandoned his forty-four-year marriage, which seems to me a little like shipwreck survivors diving off the lifeboat within sight of land. Five years later, he was alone when a doctor delivered the news that he had Alzheimer's, and though I don't know what kind of cargo he lugged around with him those forty-four years, I can't help wondering who would have been there to nurse him and love him had he stuck around when everything within yelled "Run!"

There is something that may sound dull and old-fashioned, but I think we lose before we've started if we don't introduce it to our children. It is the beautiful concept of faithfulness. I have seen it in the faces of the aged, in a glance or a wink. It can start today, because God's mercies are new every morning. It can start when we sit across from our spouse and choose thanksgiving over griping and forgiveness over holding a grudge.

For my wife, it happens when I admit to her that I'd like to pick out some clothes that make me look "younger," and she doesn't roll her eyes at all, just helps me pick them out. A few weeks ago I told her I'd love to have one of those little red convertibles, and instead of waking up in the middle of the night to put Super Glue on my eyelids, she bought me a little model Corvette at Costco for $12.99.

I Proposed in a Chain Letter

*For marriage to be a success, every woman and
every man should have his or her own bathroom.*

CATHERINE ZETA-JONES

෧෧

*A good marriage is like an incredible retirement fund.
You put everything you have into it during your productive
life, and over the years it turns from silver to gold to platinum.*

WILLARD SCOTT

My wife is eight months older than me. No one believes this. You see the two of us together and you'll see why. One of us looks like George Burns, and the other like, well, like my wife. Ramona was standing in the grocery store the other day, and a lady asked, "Is it your dad who writes those books?"

"Yes," she replied, past a widening smile.

One day my wife looked at my white hair and said, "When I agreed to grow old with you, I didn't mean this rapidly."

Last August we celebrated twenty-five years of married life—most of them good ones. When I was a boy, the only people celebrating twenty-fifth anniversaries were very old people with ample wrinkles, high fore-heads, and starchy clothing—people who were so old they had reached their forties and needed help getting up stairs. Most of them seemed happy. Others looked like love was a dream and marriage was the alarm clock.

I consider ours a miracle marriage, especially when you consider that I proposed to Ramona via chain letter. This is what it said:

Dear Ramona Bjorndal,

Do not throw this letter away! This chain letter was started by my ancestors just after the Great Flood and it has NEVER EVER BEEN BROKEN! To keep the chain going, all you have to do is marry me. This will include providing decent meals, clean laun-dry, and lots of love for the next sixty years. In return, you will receive my undying devotion, occasional flowers, chocolate, and access to my car keys until death do us part. If you break the chain, you will be destined to live a life of misery and boredom, much like the math class we are now sitting in.

It was pretty clever stuff for a tenth grader, don't you think? And four years later, when I summoned the courage to show it to her, she laughed. And agreed to marry me anyway.

In August, we took leave of our teenagers and returned to the same hotel where we first shared a pillow all those years ago. The staff, impressed that a couple could stay together this long, couldn't spoil us enough. They wheeled in complimentary chocolates, chocolate-dipped strawberries, and a large bottle of champagne on ice, which we mistook for bubble bath and used accordingly.

As we dove into the chocolates, we talked about some pretty sweet years together. I suppose there are a thousand reasons we still share the same phone number and address; here are just a few:

1. We sweat the small stuff. Early on I left mud on the carpet and whiskers in the sink. I even left my underwear where it landed. I'm learning to take care of the small things before they become big ones. If I'm last out of bed, I make it. (I have done this twice.) If I'm late for supper, I call home. We go to bed at the same time even when I'm not tired, and I kiss her lips before I shave each morning. Just the other day, I even—drum roll, please—located the laundry hamper.

2. We golf together. Ramona enjoys golf about as much as I enjoy shopping for curtain fabric. Still, she comes along sometimes and cheers as I putt. This is annoying, but I love having her there. One of our anniversaries was even celebrated, at her suggestion, on a golf course. Perhaps that's why I find it easier to do the dishes, vacuum carpets, bathe the dog, or move furniture whenever she asks—which is often in the middle of the night.

3. We eat together. Whenever possible, we eat meals together, believing mealtime to be an enormously important time of the day. We even cook together, though we seldom agree on recipes. Before we had children we were often invited out for meals. (We were invited out only once when our three were small. I imagine that the gracious elderly couple who did the inviting are still chipping food off their walls.) We would be eating some new dish, and Ramona would be savoring each mouthful. "I need to get this recipe," she would say. And I would be looking at her with horror because I was stuffing bite-sized pieces of sandwich in my pockets whenever our host wasn't looking. And so we worked out a signal. When we're invited out and she asks

for a recipe, and I don't like the food, I say, "It's tasty." Tasty is code for "this tomato flambé tastes exactly like a skunk swam through it. Don't, under any circumstances, bring home the recipe."

4. We practice forgiveness. One of my favorite quotes comes from Frederick Buechner: "Of the seven deadly sins, anger is possibly the most fun. To lick your wounds, to smack your lips over grievances long past, to roll over your tongue the prospect of bitter confrontations still to come, to savor to the last toothsome morsel both the pain you are given and the pain you are giving back—in many ways it is a feast fit for a king. The chief drawback is that what you are wolfing down is yourself. The skeleton at the feast is you."[11] My brother Tim likes to put it more simply: "Not forgiving is like drinking rat poison, then standing around waiting for the rat to die."

5. We travel together. Whenever possible, Ramona goes along with me on a trip. Sure, it costs money, and I haven't had a window seat in years, but I'd like to grow old with someone who doesn't just share my money, she shares my memories.

6. We left no alternatives. The first three years of our marriage were miserable. Until I got a divorce. A divorce from loving myself and seeking my own way. I was reading the book of Galatians one night when I stumbled on the verse, "I no longer live, but Christ lives in me" (2:20), and the most profound thought hit me: *If I am dead, and Christ lives in me, can my wife see Him there?* (Here's a tip: If you want to have a miserable marriage, don't read the Bible.) Finding the right person, I have since discovered, is less important than

being the right person. The happiest married people I know discovered early on that the "better" comes after the "worse."

7. We pray together. This was one of Ramona's first wishes for our marriage. And after reading that Bible verse, I came to honor it. We've since discovered that couples who pray together regularly report "the most satisfying marriages of all."[12] Lately, Ramona and I have been thanking God at night for His amazing grace. For taking two selfish kids who hardly knew how to spell *love* and pulling them close to Himself and to each other.

On our way to the hotel I turned on the radio to hear Huey Lewis singing, "I'm happy to be stuck with you." I tapped my toes (this irritates my wife when I'm driving) and smiled. But glue or chains don't hold a marriage together. A hundred tiny threads do. Threads like trust, commitment, kindness, humility, gentleness, respect, and finding the laundry hamper.

As we checked in, I told our hostess the significance of this day. Her eyes grew wide. "Wow," she said, "that's a long time with one person!"

"Yes," I replied with a grin, "but it would have been a whole lot longer without her."

I told you years ago, Ethel, to lay off the Botox.

The Great Big Marriage Quiz

When you see a married couple walking down the street,
the one that's a few steps ahead is the one that's mad.

HELEN ROWLAND

∞

A happy marriage is the world's best bargain.

O. A. BATTISTA

I once wrote a humor quiz for a marriage magazine, shoved it under my parents' door, then waited to hear what would happen. Moments later I heard Mom say in the tone she used on me as a child just before I got in trouble: "Philip." Then she started to giggle. Dad snickered several times, gave two audible cackles, and was still grinning when I came to retrieve it ten minutes later.

Through the years, Mom and Dad have not modeled the perfect marriage for their children, but they've shown us how to laugh, how to celebrate, and how a happy marriage is the union of two good for-givers.

By the way, the following quiz is for married couples only, so if you are not in that category, you should skip ahead to the next chapter (assuming you aren't curious and will follow my directions willingly). The first part is…

For Guys Only

How much do you know about the state of your marriage and the gal you wake up beside each morning? How she thinks. What makes her tick. And why "Fine" isn't good enough when she asks how your day went. Take this quiz and find out.

1. The movie your wife will most want you to rent on your next anniversary is:
   a. Lethal Auto Combat 6 in 3D.
   b. Something with foreign people talking foreign with words at the bottom.
   c. Anything so romantic you won't care if you see the end of the movie.

2. The thing your wife loves whispered in her ear is:
   a. Quotations by Homer.
   b. Quotations by Homer Simpson.
   c. Sweet somethings.

3. For your tenth anniversary, the gift your wife will want more than anything is:
   a. That plaid Barcalounger for two with his and hers cup holders.
   b. What? We have an anniversary? When?
   c. Chocolate, flowers, and your undivided attention (to her, not the chocolate).

4. How would you describe yourself as a father?
   a. What? We have children?
   b. I spend time with my kids when I can find them.
   c. I'm working on it.

5. How often do you have marital relations?

    a. When I say so, woman.

    b. We haven't had the relatives over since the Thanksgiving Jell-O Fiasco.

    c. I'd love to answer that question, but my wife and I haven't seen each other in an hour and a half.

6. Your wife asks you, "What were Humphrey Bogart's famous words to the lovely Ingrid Bergman in the romantic film *Casablanca*?" You respond:

    a. "Go ahead, make my day."

50 Ways to Keep Your Lover

1. Morning kisses.
2. Evening walks.
3. Leave flirtatious messages on his or her voice mail. Be sure to dial correctly.
4. Maintain a stubborn commitment to each other.
5. Ladies: Don't vacuum during football games.
6. Men: Don't eat onions unless she does.
7. Love when you don't feel like it.
8. Read together.
9. Laugh together.
10. Accept blame.
11. Share entrées.
12. Be nice.
13. Lower your expectations.
14. Never purposely embarrass each other.
15. Never equate success with stuff.
16. Hold hands.
17. Ride bikes.
18. Ladies: Tell him you like him better with less hair.
19. Men: Tell her you like her haircut.
20. Window shop.
21. Give backrubs.
22. Trade footrubs.
23. View infidelity for what it is: poison.
24. Take marriage seriously. Work at it.

  b. "First rule of Fight Club is you do not talk about Fight Club."

  c. "Here's lookin' at you, kid."

7. The last thing you said to your wife today before you left for work was:

  a. "The kids are up and they're eating bowls of Mega Choco Zingo Puffs with salad tongs."

  b. "Yikes! You may want to put some concealer on that."

  c. "Can't wait to see you tonight."

8. On your fortieth anniversary, the song title that best describes your sex life will be:

25. Visit iTunes together and download music from your dating days.

26. Remember your first date.

27. Laugh together.

28. Cry together.

29. Be givers.

30. Make good, positive friends and keep them.

31. Be accountable.

32. Learn to talk.

33. Ladies: Don't subsist on romance novels.

34. Guys: Guard your heart.

35. Say sorry.

36. Say thank you.

37. Encourage.

38. Forgive.

39. Watch *Jaws* together. Better yet, watch it without your feet in a hot tub.

40. Send his favorite book to the author for an autograph.

41. Hold each other tight.

42. Give each other space.

43. Attend church regularly.

44. Disagree while smiling.

45. Drop grudges.

46. Make up.

47. Never mix evening news and bedtime.

48. Draw close to God.

49. End the day with prayer.

50. Remember the day will come when our clocks will stop and our 401(k) plans will expire, but our footprints will remain.

a. "I Say a Little Prayer"

b. "Yesterday"

c. "(Oh, What a Feeling When We're) Dancing on the Ceiling"

How to Score

If you chose only the "a" answers, your chances of scoring are not that good. Please go to the *C* section in the yellow pages and look up *Counselor.* If you gravitated mostly to the "b" responses, your funny bone is in good working order, but you could still use a little help. Please take an aspirin and read the rest of this book in the morning. If you chose "c" five or more times, thanks for taking this quiz on your honeymoon. Sounds like some tenderness, a good sense of humor, and a servant's heart are keeping your marriage fresh. Now it's time to show the rest of this chapter to your wife.

For Gals Only

These eight questions are intended to help you discover how well you really know the guy in your life. You may want to fill it out with your husband. Then again, you may want to take it into the bathroom, lock the door, and let him wonder what you're snickering about.

1. If I leave my husband alone for the weekend, his diet will consist of:

    a. Vegetables, fruits, and organic granola.

    b. Actually, he could very well starve to death.

    c. Stuff he finds in the sofa.

2. The gift my husband most loves to receive on his birthday:

    a. Socks. Lots and lots of socks.

    b. Flowers and cute underwear.

c. Cheesecake. Served by me—wearing only socks.

3. After a tough day at work my husband loves it when I:

   a. Gripe about the way his belt doesn't match his shoes.

   b. Gripe about the way my belt doesn't match my shoes.

   c. Ask about the big game.

4. My husband's nickname for our bed is:

   a. Old Lumpy

   b. Headache Generator

   c. The Hibachi

5. After he uses the facilities at our house, the toilet seat is:

   a. Don't ask.

   b. Glued in the upright position.

   c. Like our marriage—sometimes up, sometimes down.

6. Outside the bedroom, my husband's favorite activity is:

   a. Holding my purse outside the fitting room while I try on pantsuits in multiples of five.

   b. Going to the video store with me to help decide between all the Julia Roberts chick flicks.

   c. Figuring out ways to get us back in the bedroom.

7. How do you and your husband settle differences of opinion?

   a. We don't disagree. I'm the queen.

   b. He spends the night on the plaid Barcalounger.

   c. A good discussion, some black forest cake, and…well, none of your beeswax.

8. On our twenty-fifth anniversary, the song title that will best describe our sex life will be:

   a. The theme from *Mission: Impossible*

   b. "Wishin' and Hopin'"

   c. "Oh, What a Night"

How to Score

Give yourself one point each time you selected "c." If you did so at least five times, it is now safe to come out of the bathroom and show your husband what you've been laughing about. If you circled only "a" or "b" answers, stay in there and take the test again. Collect one hundred bonus points if you smiled at least twice during this quiz and one thousand air miles if you resolved afresh to love the guy God gave you.

20

Day of Rejoicing

*A boy becomes an adult three years before his parents
think he does, and about two years after he thinks he does.*

LEWIS B. HERSHEY

O ur eldest child has grown up fast, graduating from high school
and considering what's next. We were on the golf course one day
when an oil tycoon strolled over and offered him a job at ten
times the salary I earned at his age. I couldn't believe he didn't
take it. When I asked him why, he said he wanted to do something bigger with his life than make money. He said he'd been listening to me
preach and that I had advised people to do something they loved and
they wouldn't have to work a day in their lives.

"I said that?"

He smiled. "You did."

And so Steve enrolled in Bible college, a decision that has his mother
and me rejoicing and sniffling and clutching our wallets all at once. The
price for Bible college has not decreased since I attended in the latter half
of the last century, but I assured him it would not be a problem. We
would sell his little brother into slavery to pay for the first semester. (I'm
kidding. I did not sell my son. Please do not write me letters about this.)

One hot fall morning he set out for the Montana mountains to
begin Explore, a wilderness leadership program "where Christian leaders

are born, where apologetics meet practical teaching in a pristine wilderness setting." I have the sneaking suspicion Explore is really an excuse to go on an extended camping trip while getting to know women.

And I'll admit to something else. Bible college wasn't on my agenda for this boy. I've checked Fortune 500 and *Money* magazine. There are very few ministers, missionaries, and camp directors listed there. I will reach retirement age in twenty years. Who will pay for my medication?

That morning the girls in the program watched as Steve's mother kissed his cheek and I hugged him good-bye. He's never been a hugger, but he didn't wriggle away. There were no tears in his eyes, and certainly none in mine. In fact, I couldn't have been happier. It was a holiday. The sky was blue. The air was warm. The clouds were nonthreatening. I would go home and hoist a ginger ale, then cut the grass.

Pushing our old weed whacker along, I considered all the reasons I was happy to have this kid out of the house. These were just a start:

- No more toothpaste on our bathroom door.
- No more mold growing beneath his bed.
- His music can keep someone else up now.
- I can find my ties, my tools, and my remote control.
- No more stepping in remnants of last night's yogurt snack.
- Or tripping over clothes on the floor.
- We will save roughly four hundred dollars per month on groceries. Two hundred in milk alone.
- No more adjusting the seat and mirror when I drive the car.
- No more phone calls interrupting my work: "Dad, let's go golfing."
- No more flopping on our bed at night to tell us of his day.

I was free.

That night we crawled into bed, Ramona and I, the lawn neatly trimmed, the house cleaned, the back porch swept, and she said, "Aren't you glad Steve wants to serve God? We've prayed that he would since he was knee-high to a Lego block."

How could I disagree? I started reciting my list, but Ramona had drifted off already, so I lay there with my hands behind my thinning hairdo, gazing up at the stippled ceiling. My smile had subsided a little. It wasn't like I'd been baptized in lemon juice, but you get the picture.

Most nights Steve brushes his teeth outside our bedroom door. If the door is open, he comes in. Boys are easy to talk to when there's toothpaste in their mouth. Suddenly I missed those talks. I missed him pretending to wipe out as he came thumping down the stairs, just to see the horrified looks on our faces. I missed the music he would crank up about 11 p.m. in the room below us. Even if it sounded like someone killing chickens with a jackhammer. I missed him rolling on the floor with the dog and sometimes me. I missed standing at the fridge together about midnight talking about our day and wondering where Mom hid the mayonnaise.

Grandpa and Grandma missed him too. "We pray for him every night," they said.

Even the dog missed Steve. I went looking for her one night, thinking the hound was lost. She was lying on Steve's bed, her tail in the downward position. And try as I might to be brave and manly and a positive thinker Robert H. Schuller would admire, there were tears on my cheeks there in the dark.

I know there are far worse things than hugging your firstborn good-bye as he goes off to Bible college, but I missed my son.

"Lord," I prayed, "take care of this boy. I know he was on loan, but we got pretty attached to him. Wherever he is and wherever he goes, go with him."

And I thanked God that He loaned us two more kids. I'm so glad they're around. They're bright kids. I think they'll make good lawyers. They can buy my medication.

21

The Longing

There is not a heart but has its moments
of longing, yearning for something better, nobler,
holier than it knows now.

HENRY WARD BEECHER

൭൭

The older you get, the more it takes to fill your heart
with wonder…and only God is big enough to do that.

RAVI ZACHARIAS

Sometimes friends ask questions that make me smile. Like "If it's a TV set, why do you only get one of them?" But other questions stop me dead in my tracks; some even make me think. Like the one my friend Andy Andersen was honest enough to ask one muggy June night in Florida.

Back in 1993, Andy was enjoying life as a U.S. Navy commander, serving as executive officer of a naval aviation squadron out of Jacksonville, Florida. His Cary Grant smile and gentle strength endeared him to those he led. One day a sailor began asking for financial advice, and Andy responded with a few questions of his own—about the man's own philosophy of life and debt. Soon the two were lost in discussion, barely realizing that twenty others were eavesdropping on their conversation. Andy invited them to join in. "They were begging for more information," he says. "Some had creditors beating down their doors, others were watching money problems ruin their marriages."

Andy decided to put together a financial management seminar and soon found himself speaking to other squadrons in the Jacksonville area. News of the popular workshops spread as far as Washington DC, where he was asked to join the board of a billion-dollar corporation and launch the navy's financial management program on C-SPAN live from the Pentagon.

By 1998 he was on top of the world, promoted to captain and serving as an executive assistant to the secretary of defense, Bill Cohen. But deep inside there was a nagging emptiness. "I was the first guy with a lampshade on my head at parties," he recalls. "I went to church but had no relationship with Christ." One April night he uttered a desperate prayer asking for some kind of sign. He drifted off, and the sign arrived in a vivid dream. "I awoke in a huge cave with a crack in the ceiling and beams of light shining down on an old rugged cross. I could see a man on the cross, his head covered in blood and sweat. I approached the cross and saw that it was Christ, that He had been crucified and was dead. Suddenly His eyes opened, His hand pulled away from the wood and stretched out to me. He said, 'I am God. I love you. I did this for you.' "

Andy awoke knowing he would never be the same.

In October he noticed my book *Making Life Rich Without Any Money* in a Pentagon bookstore and read it on a flight to his twenty-five-year high school reunion. According to Andy, God used the book "to change my life forever." He began writing me letters, asking honest and refreshing questions that young followers of Christ long to know. The first was this: "Will Jesus still love me if I buy a Mercedes convertible?"

I smiled at his question, then wrote him back. "Jesus will never leave you," I told him. "He will love you even if you drive a Ford." But I asked him to consider what he could do with the money he saved if he were to buy a used car. I reminded him of the message of the book: that money makes a lousy master but a great servant.

The day Andy received my letter, he was walking past a bulletin board when a picture caught his eye. A red Mustang convertible, good as new, but half the price. "I'd always wanted a Mustang," he told me. "Besides, it was thirty thousand dollars less than the silver Mercedes." So he bought it.

Andy began investing in others. And God began to bless him.

Soon he was selected to command the navy's largest squadron—over twelve hundred sailors. "I knew I had a wonderful opportunity to impact all those lives," he recalls. "I wanted to show them that happiness has nothing to do with the materialistic pursuits that kill the joy of so many." He modified his financial seminar, basing it on my book. I sued him and made millions. Okay, not really. But as Andy warned listeners about the pitfalls of a stressful and selfish society, the seminar had a profound effect. "People were happier and more motivated. They felt a greater sense of worth. Within six months we had a complete reversal in squadron performance." He even began selling my book afterward for a nominal fee, watching thousands of them go into the hands of navy personnel who wouldn't dream of opening a church door. Today Andy's platform continues to grow as he conducts his workshops all over the country.

One muggy June evening as we sampled seafood together in a restaurant near Jacksonville, Florida, Andy talked of those days. "I worked with a few ladies you may have heard of," he grinned. "Monica Lewinsky and Linda Tripp. Most of what I heard I didn't believe—until I read it in the newspaper." While the world learned of the scandal brought on by selfishness, money, power, and lust, Andy felt inspired to up the stakes of his workshop, teaching the lasting benefits of integrity, faithfulness, and helping others. But as he encountered the stresses and strains of middle age, Captain Andersen admitted that he was having a crisis of faith.

Leaning toward me, he asked, "Why are you still a Christian?"

I was midway through a fistful of shrimp from the buffet, but I managed to ask, "What do you mean?"

"Well, since I gave my life to Christ, things have gotten worse. I've been beaten up and robbed. I'm being sued for no good reason. Things aren't great on so many fronts. What about you? Why are you still a Christian?"

I'm usually silent in the face of such questions. Or I try to hide behind people who are brighter than I—and thankfully my high school buddy Kevin was along on this trip. Kevin spoke wisely of the resurrection of Christ, of the lack of viable alternatives. Andy's wife, Cindy, was there too. She talked of the change in her own life. And then the three of them looked at me because I am wise and witty and would surely have an answer.

I ate more shrimp. I mentioned the fact that no other belief system had satisfied my craving for truth. I talked of people in my life who have no earthly reason to rejoice but whose lives are filled with joy. But what came next from my mouth was not what I intended.

"You know," I said, toying with my fork, "I've traveled in limousines, stayed in the finest hotels, eaten the fattest shrimp. And I've had this strange feeling I can't properly explain. I remember one night in particular, sitting on a powdery beach in Maui—an absolute paradise for a Canadian. My children were throwing the Frisbee nearby and actually getting along. I kid you not, this happened. I was holding the hand of the one person in all the world that I love the most."

"Who was that?" interrupted Kevin.

"The girl I've been stark raving mad about since the age of fifteen,"

I answered. "You know, the thought hit me as I held her hand: *This is as good as it gets down here, but it's not enough. There must be more than this.*"

Surprisingly, Andy and his wife leaned forward. I told them of C. S. Lewis, the brilliant thinker who went from avowed atheist to follower of Christ. "Lewis wrote, 'If I find in myself a desire which no experience in this world can satisfy, the most probable explanation is that I was made for another world.' "

"I've never heard it put that way," said Andy. "That's really what led me to Christ."

The Middle Ages often usher in a time of doubt. What I want are answers, and sometimes I just get questions. But sometimes it's the questions that keep me moving forward, stumbling heavenward.

Deep within each of us is a voice that we will hear if we just get quiet enough to listen. A voice telling us that nothing in this world will entirely keep its promise, that what we want most cannot be had down here. The best marriage, the sweetest salary, the flashiest car—nothing will ever entirely satisfy this longing.

On my bulletin board is the picture of the man with the Cary Grant smile, grinning up at me from his red Mustang convertible, his faithful Labrador retriever, Dusty, by his side. Andy's picture reminds me never to stop asking questions. It reminds me of integrity and truth, of a longing for Home.

22

How's Your Stuffometer?

I'll tell you how to beat the gambling in Las Vegas.
When you get off the airplane, walk right into the propeller.
HENNY YOUNGMAN

∽

I do not read advertisements.
I would spend all my time wanting things.
FRANZ KAFKA

One morning our remaining son, Jeff, held up the newspaper and said, "Dad, look!" It was a full-page advertisement for a wide-screen HDTV. A TV that would fit perfectly along our south basement wall. Bold numbers were scrawled across the TV: $44. "Dad, look, we can buy one."

I said, "Read the little print below the big print. That's forty-four bucks a month until the year 2349." His eyes grew wider as he read the small print. His dad was right.

I thought to myself, *Of all the bad habits we are teaching our young, few are worse than the notion that they can have it all now. That good things come to those who pounce. And borrow. And max out their credit cards.*

We're paying our Visa bills with our MasterCards so we can impress people we don't like with things we don't need and get air miles that we can't use thanks to blackout dates. When money enters the equation, our brains short-circuit. We get dumber than a sack of hammers. I once saw an advertising slogan in a bank: "We will lend you enough money to get you completely out of debt."

For the first time in world history, Americans and Canadians are spending more than we make. But what culture of any worth loves its economy more than its children? Remember the word *wait*?

Flying into a beautiful city in California, I looked out my window at all the massive houses. Many of the garages would dwarf entire houses of thirty years ago. The average American residence now has three more rooms than the homes of twenty years ago. I think I know why. We need bigger houses because we're having so many kids. Whoops. Maybe not. Fifty years ago the average couple had twenty-seven children, give or take a dozen. They had to issue nametags. Not anymore. The average couple now has 1.7 children. My daughter points at my son and says, "Him. He's the point seven!"

We need bigger houses because we want to impress others, and we'd like more room for our stuff. We've never had more stuff in the history of mankind or womankind. We've become stuffaholics. We measure success with a stuffometer. We have pants that talk. They're made in Great Britain. They simply say, "Zip me" (maybe some of us need these). We have cell phones that work underwater. What an answer to prayer! We have clocks to shine the time on our ceilings in the middle of the night. They're an insomniac's dream. At some point each December most of us, me included, scratch our heads and ask, "What do we get for the person who has everything?" Here's a radical answer: How about nothing? How about an arm around their shoulder, a kind word, and a glass of iced tea together?

New York writer Liz Perle McKenna decided on a most unusual way to declutter her life. For her fortieth birthday party, she invited friends to come to her house and take one thing of their choosing.[13] Most of us are thinking, I'd sure like to be her friend.

Would someone please explain to me who convinced us that we would be happier chasing stuff than enjoying relationships? Because that's what we're doing. We have more shopping malls than high schools now. We spend more money on pet food than missions. As Richard Swenson says, "The good life now means the *goods* life."

But how can we know if we have enough stuff? Thankfully, advertisers, who really care about us, have a handy little form we can fill out. It's called:

The Stuffometer Questionnaire

(Sponsored by the same guys who brought you the slogan "You're worth it.")

- How much stuff do you have right now?
- WHAT? Are you COMPLETELY INSANE? Do you have sawdust for brains? It's not NEARLY enough.
- We'll be right over.

The advertising industry is waging a nonstop bombardment on our minds. They spend billions creating discontent, convincing us that we are miserable creatures. *You poor thing. You do not have a water filter for your cat dish. How do you live without one? Buy one today, and we'll throw in a free nose-hair trimmer for your gerbil.*

I saw an ad on TV recently for a beautiful luxury car. A well-oiled narrator said softly, "The only cure for temptation is to surrender to it."

And I thought, *Now there's a noble creed to live by. Does that mean I can scratch your car?* I was tempted.

Buick once tried to sell us with the slogan "Buick: Something to believe in." Hmmm…we can now worship at the First Church of the Buick. Take out your Owner's Manuals, and let's sing together from page 33.

Then there's the ad with a guy holding a beer can. Without slurring his words, he says, "It doesn't get any better than this." Pardon me? If this is as good as it gets, we're a miserable lot.

I prefer the old ads. Like the one I once saw in a newspaper. It said, "Used Cars. Why go elsewhere to be cheated? Come here first." Here are a few more of my favorites:

Free: Farm kittens. Ready to eat.
Our sofa seats the whole mob—and it's made of 100% Italian
      leather.
For Sale: NordicTrack. $300. Hardly used. Call Chubby at…
Kittens, eight weeks old. Seeking good Christian home.

And so we are left with a choice. Store up for ourselves treasures on earth where they need fixing, storing, insuring, painting, maintaining, rustproofing, and constant attention. Or we can follow Jesus' advice in Matthew 6:20 and store up for ourselves "treasures in heaven, where moth and rust do not destroy, and where thieves do not break in and steal."

Here are a few ideas to start us down the road to debt-free living and a place called Peace.

- ◑ Take a child by the hand and go for a walk. Make sure it's your child.
- ◑ If you are in debt: (a) make a budget, (b) pour lighter fluid on your credit cards, (c) light them, and (d) then

use cash for all purchases. Ask older people about cash; they know what it is.

⊚ Buy bottled water every twenty-three years. At the corner store near us, you can buy "a taste of paradise" water from Fiji on sale for $1.50 per bottle or $11.36 a gallon. We spend less than one-third of a cent per gallon for water that comes out of a tap twelve steps from our bed. If you buy two bottles of water a day, you can save $1,095 a year by taking along your own plastic bottle and filling it up with tap water—water that most of the world would give just about anything to drink (by the way, Pepsi recently admitted that Aquafina comes from…are you ready?…a tap).

⊚ Boycott Starbucks. If you buy five lattes per week for a year, you will spend $1,040. Stop it. If you need caffeine, buy $40 worth of beans at Safeway and suck on five a day. My boss does this, and I rarely catch him napping.

⊚ Get married and stay married. According to a report by the *Journal of Sociology*[14] (get ready, big surprise ahead), marriage actually *increases* your emotional and financial health. "Scrapping a marriage robs you of wealth," claims the study. After surveying nine thousand people, they found that divorce reduces a person's wealth by 77 percent and that married people increased their wealth about 4 percent per year.

⊚ Avoid frugal-living books. I picked one up recently, and here is a sampling of the brilliant advice: Buy a goat for milk! (I kid you not—no pun intended.) Invite the grandparents to visit—they'll bring gifts for the kids! Don't take your children shopping! Cut open your toothpaste tube!

Reuse your trash bags! The book was on sale for twenty bucks!

- ◉ Support your church, missionaries you know, needy people, and organizations that are making a difference.
- ◉ Leave the TV off during dinner. Don't hurry through dinner. If you do, it might hurry through you.
- ◉ Teach your children that we need money to buy things. If we don't have money, we can't buy things.
- ◉ Put memories ahead of money.
- ◉ Meditate on Micah 6:8, Revised Materialist's Edition: "What does the Lord require of you? That you act justly, that you love mercy, and that you run, run, run like a gerbil." No! That you "walk humbly with your God."

When Steve came home for a weekend, the five of us sat in the living room talking. For some reason the issue of money surfaced, so we reminded our teens of our fiscal philosophy. We told them we're investing in organizations that are focused on eternity. We told them we're not leaving a bunch of cash behind, so they'd better get jobs. I told them what was in our will. It says this: "We, being of sound mind, spent all our money."

In fact, the last check I write will be to the undertaker. And it's gonna bounce.

Harry thought no one cared he was alive.
Then he missed a mortgage payment.

23

The Trouble with Success

I don't know why fortune smiles on some.
And lets the rest go free.

THE EAGLES, "THE SAD CAFE"

☙

Learn to say no. It will be of more
use to you than the ability to read Latin.

CHARLES HADDON SPURGEON

I am always honored and surprised when asked to speak at writers' conferences. Here is what I tell them:

A few years back I wrote a book called *Making Life Rich Without Any Money*, and it made me lots of money. There were book royalties, which were modest and nice. Then came the speaking engagements. A lady pulled me aside after one of them and invited me to join her agency. My speeches on being rich without money would fetch five figures a talk (without decimal points), she said, a sum triple the advance on the book.

I thought of Al Gore, who warns of global warming and then takes a stretch limousine to catch his private plane home to sit in a heated pool in his Tennessee mansion that consumes twenty times the electricity used by the average American house.[15]

I thanked the lady but turned her down out of principle. Then I kicked myself all the way home.

My wife, who practices what I preach, reminded me that it's tough to teach about simplicity while stockpiling stuff. That you can't lip-sync at life. "We don't own anything," she said, "it's all on loan. We have a bigger purpose on the planet." Stuff like that. I plugged my ears and hummed real loud.

Part of why I would like to have bundles of thousand-dollar bills beneath my mattress is that I grew up below what our government calls the poverty line. And though I've heard that money won't buy you happiness, I'd like to research the notion for myself.

A dozen years ago my first book landed on a bestseller list. My elementary school teachers prepared me for numerous things, but not for success. If asked who might become a successful writer, they would have singled out girls with horn-rimmed spectacles who sat upright in their chairs, finishing assignments on time. My report cards prepared me for failure. But success? It is worse, my friends.

First off, a publicist calls to inform you that complete strangers want to talk with you. They want you to be on the radio (what will I say?) or on television (what will I wear?). She tells you that they're couriering you stuff like plane tickets to different cities; you, who gets lost driving to the grocery store. They promise to pay for everything, though—everything but twenty-four-hour limousine service and movies in your hotel room. (Someone else already tried this. My lawyer said I can't tell you his name.) Next up, the publisher swiftly couriers you another book contract with an advance three times the amount of the first one, and you sign before they retract the thing and tell you they were joking.

When the check arrives, so does a book cover awaiting your approval.

You laugh so hard that vital organs begin to hurt because you haven't written a single word of the book yet. While you're still midway through writing the first chapter, a marketing guru calls to tell you how many copies bookstores have already ordered, and you begin to experience respiratory problems. Expectations aren't so great when they are someone else's.

Reporters conduct interviews. It is intoxicating. They ask you what it's like to be an author. "I write much because I am paid little," you say, and they like that. Your poverty endears you to them. You tell them that the garbage can is a writer's best friend, that writing a book is like driving a car at night: You can't see very far, but you follow the lights. You tell them that writing is the hardest way of earning a living, with the possible exception of loading hand grenades.

Fellow writers ask you to review their manuscripts and offer advice or, better yet, write a note of recommendation to a publisher of your choosing. You write them back: "This is great stuff. I'm sorry I have no time to read it." They print your first sentence on the covers of their books. You ask a friend for advice, and he grows quiet. "I'm not boasting," you say, "I'm having a panic attack." And you are.

An editor calls. He is flying in to meet with you about more projects. Others discover your phone number. Accountants. Agents. Critics. Magazine editors. Hopeful authors. Financial planners. Fans in prison. Little kids who want your picture. The tax audit guy. *No man can serve two masters,* you think. *But how about twenty-three? Surely that's possible.* But it isn't. It's like you are a bag of sand, and someone cut a hole in the bottom. You are dying of easy accessibility.

Dear people call you late at night to discuss your new book and how it relates to their unique problems. Could you drive to their house and help them with their marriage? You tell them you would, but you've hardly seen your own wife the past week. Still, they find your address and drive long distances to tell you of their childhoods, their failures, their sins. You advise them to talk with their minister. "He's tired of me," they say.

You cut your hair, and people write to discuss the new style. You find yourself standing before audiences of thousands—you, who couldn't speak up in Sunday school for fear of ridicule. You go to sleep complaining to your wife of chest pains and she says, "Just say no. It was good enough for Nancy Reagan."

And then one day you wake up and smell the decaf. It comes in the form of a beautiful letter. "My life was changed forever… My family and I are following Christ after reading your book." And you get down on your knees and repent of your whining and give thanks to Almighty God for the privilege and the pains and the joys of being a writer. You thank Him for the true friends who stick around—even in the midst of your success. For a wife who gives all your money away. A woman who advises you to take a couple of those speaking engagements a year and use the money to help others.

And you thank God that throughout history He hasn't always used the ones who please Him; He uses whomever He pleases. Even you.

24

Mondays with James

*I come from a family where gravy
is considered a beverage.*

ERMA BOMBECK

Twice a week James Enns and I enjoy lunch together after exercising for twenty minutes on machines intended for gerbils. The meal is really an incentive. We can't stand the thought of exercise without immediate reward, and so we hold it in front of us, like the weekend on a Monday. Recompense gives purpose to our exercise.

When we were children, we ran ten miles a day without knowing it, kicking a ball or being chased by Mr. Pike for sampling his raspberries. But not anymore. No one plays sports these days unless their parents organize it. There's too much on television.

James and I talked for some time about beginning an exercise program but were distracted by other things. After all, we are busy guys. James is a year away from completing his PhD from Cambridge. My schedule keeps me weeks away from a nervous breakdown. Then one day I stepped on the scales and thought to myself, *Hey, I'd like to live to be fifty-five and have all parts of my body stop moving when I do.*

And so I called James, who agreed that I needed help and that he would join me.

Contrary to what I say in chapter 34, exercise is a good thing and we're wise to grab some of it each day. Also, we should eat right. It won't kill us. Those who subsist on french fries and Cheetos risk having a heart attack each time the toast pops up. I once saw pictures in *National Geographic* of a somewhat wizened Russian man who, though he had no documents to prove it, estimated his age to be 120 years, give or take a few. He said the secret to his longevity was a pound of bacon at breakfast, a shot of vodka at lunchtime, and lots and lots of unfiltered cigarettes throughout the day.

There are three things I know for sure about this:

1. He is the exception.
2. He was probably lying.
3. He was probably twenty-nine.

The thing I like about exercise is the same thing I like about banging my head against a stone wall: It feels good when I stop. But it's worth it for those meals we enjoy together in the little sub sandwich shop near the exercise room.

We are unlikely friends, James and I. The similarity in our sandwiches ends with the chicken and the mayo. He loves red peppers and jalapeños and Mother-in-Law hot sauce. I get heartburn just watching him order. James dislikes pickles. This is a spiritual problem he has. I eat pickles by the fistful. He prefers Coke with ice. I go without.

James is an Anglican. I am Evangelical Free. He is a scholar. I am not. He can debate circles around me. It's like Plato and Steve Martin doing lunch. Steve knows that the next best thing to being wise is to hang out with someone who is. I try to keep up as James discusses the theological ramifications of the big bang theory, but since I personally invented attention deficit disorder back in 1966, the Big Bang

makes me think of Mr. Big chocolate bars, which reminds me that I
didn't get my wife anything for her birthday on Saturday, which is the
day of the week we were married back in 1982, the very year the
Washington Redskins won the Super Bowl, which makes me think of
quarterbacks, which makes me wonder if I have enough spare change
for coffee this afternoon.

I interrupt. "Did you hear about the crisis in Colombia?"

He frowns. "You've got ranch dressing on your nose," he says.

Real friends do that. They point out mustard on your mustache and
tea leaves in your teeth and inconsistencies in your spiritual life. James
and I don't agree on every little point, so mostly we stick to the ones that
matter. We bow together before each meal, like saplings that have
learned the best way to deal with the north wind, asking God to bless
and protect our wives and children and to make us a blessing too.

"Lord, in a world where many go hungry, we thank You for food.
Where many walk alone, we thank You for friends. Where many long
for healing, we thank You for hope."

What began as exercise has become a sacred friendship I would not
trade for all the chocolate in Hershey, Pennsylvania.

I am sometimes asked why I live in a small town where everyone
knows where you're going before you turn your signal light on. The
opportunities are golden elsewhere. And then I think of the words C. S.
Lewis wrote in a letter: "Friendship is the greatest of worldly goods.
Certainly to me it is the chief happiness of life. If I had to give a piece
of advice to a young man about a place to live, I think I should say,
'Sacrifice almost everything to live where you can be near your friends.'
I know I am very fortunate in that respect."

I wish for everyone a friend like James, a friend to hold us accountable and soak us in community.

"As iron sharpens iron, so a friend sharpens a friend," wrote Solomon in Proverbs 27:17 (NLT). Solomon must have had a James in his life. I wonder if they went out for submarine sandwiches. I imagine they were long lunches. After all, Solomon had his share of wives to pray for.

25

Brad, Britney, Bill, and Jim

Untold suffering seldom is.

FRANKLIN P. JONES

෨෨

An adventure is an inconvenience rightly considered.

G. K. CHESTERTON

Most of us do not grow one inch through success, or ease, or happy circumstances. I wish it weren't this way. I wish we learned about patience by not having to loiter in traffic. I wish we learned about peace by living in peaceful times. And more than this, I wish we learned about suffering by reading good books on the topic, books that are on the blowout table for ninety-nine cents.

I first asked my wife, Ramona, out in tenth grade[16] and soon learned that there was a 50 percent chance she was carrying around a hereditary disease known as Huntington's (HD). Though we have known for more than a decade now that she does not carry it, three of her siblings inherited this neurological disorder—her dear brother, Dennis, succumbed two Christmases ago. Today her sisters, Cynthia

and Miriam, along with their faithful husbands, Bill and Jim, are bat-
tling this awful disease, and though I don't use the term very often, I
consider the four of them to be saints, because they put others' needs
ahead of their own without telling you about it.

I fear our sad culture has replaced the servants with the stars and
that we need to refocus. If you've been unfortunate enough to read scan-
dalous headlines in the checkout line lately, I think you agree.

Recently I began receiving phone calls from the editorial staff at *Life
& Style*, a Hollywood tabloid, asking me to comment on various goings-
on in the unnatural lives of celebrities like Brad Pitt, Britney Spears, and
Angelina Jolie. I joked with them a little, then asked why they'd called
me. "You're on file as one of our experts," an editor said. I'm not sure if
she could hear me laughing.

Now, I'm old enough to get away with being cranky, so allow me a
brief rant: I have no clue about the lives of these people. I see Jessica and
Paris on the covers of magazines when I'm buying mangoes, and I know
that God loves them (Jessica and Paris, and probably the mangoes, too),
but I can't tell you a thing about their love lives. Will it help me in some
small way to know more about the feud between Rosie and Donald?
Will it better my marriage to know who broke up with whom this week?

I fear, in saying this, that someone may show up at my door and
give me a talking-to for being insubordinate, but it's a risk I'm willing to
take. Perhaps that is what aging is: sorting through what's rotten and
throwing it out.

At this time in my life, I cannot afford to be sidetracked by the triv-
ial. If I am going to write about people, there needs to be some depth,
some honor, something bordering on nobility. And that's what I've found
in the lives of these family members whose love for others propels me to
love deeper, whose laughter astounds me as much as their attitudes.

Steve Cohen is the president of The Apple of His Eye Mission

Society. Like Bill and Jim, Steve's wife, Jan, wrestles with Huntington's. And like Bill and Jim, Steve faces each new day with profound faith, a robust attitude, and a couple of much-needed chuckles.

I would love to see his face on the *National Enquirer*. "Man stays faithful to invalid wife. Maybe we should too."

Recently the Cohens celebrated thirty-one years of marriage and the fourteenth year that Jan has bravely battled Huntington's. When Steve travels throughout the country he meets people whose lives Jan's story has touched, people who are praying for them. "Please tell me how Jan is doing!" they say.

"One of the realities of HD is that our house must be as friendly as possible to Jan," Steve tells me. "This has meant a number of renovations, and most recently the overhaul of a walk-in closet so that she won't slip on something strewn on the floor. It was quite a chore, but the closet never looked so good."

With the renovation complete, Steve was downstairs with his children when they heard a thud and rushed upstairs to find Jan on the floor in the newly renovated closet. With no grab bar to steady her, she had grabbed the nearest thing she could find: the clothes. "We found her there in a mountain of clothing. Arms and legs protruding from the jumbled mass, but she was unhurt."

It was 10:30 at night when they finished rehanging the clothes, and Steve herded everyone down to the kitchen table where he announced that they were having a celebration.

"What are we celebrating?" asked the kids.

"We are celebrating the fact that the paramedics did not have to come," Steve answered. "Mom was not taken to the hospital. She did not need stitches. There is no recovery period this time, and she is not in pain. Also, we're celebrating the fact that the closet has never been cleaner."

Jan's battle with HD has helped Steve count the blessing of each day and each situation. They have discovered together that the joy of the Lord grows best in the soil of thanksgiving. "And we acknowledge God's grace and mercy—new every morning and evening, too."

A recent e-mail from my brother-in-law Jim will give you an idea of the strength God gives His saints, and the attitude we can choose:

> Miriam is doing great. Her speech is now to the point that we have difficulty understanding most of what she says. Sometimes I have to ask her to repeat herself five or six times and she starts to laugh at me. How great is that! The two phrases she says the best, and probably the most often, are "I love you" and "I'm happy." It makes my day every time. Thanks for your prayers. Isn't life amazing?

In high school I heard a sermon on what we should say when God meets us at heaven's gates and asks in His thundering Charlton Heston–ish voice why He should stoop to unlatch the door for the likes of us. I was sitting with three friends that day, and normally we were busy distracting others, reading *Alfred Hitchcock* magazines stuffed in our Bibles, or listening to transistor radios through tiny earpieces attached to wires beneath our shirts. But this day the topic sobered us enough to listen.

The preacher listed seven things we needed to say, and a host of things we would need to do on earth, before we entered the hereafter. I'm ashamed to tell you I don't remember more than one or two of them. I knew the preacher was a man who had no shortcomings; there seemed to be no reason God wouldn't open the gates wide and hug him Home. But not me. I sat there hanging my head, knowing I could never measure up.

With a few years under my belt, I have come to the conclusion that I'll be speechless when I arrive there. But if I finally find my voice and, for some reason, God asks me why He should allow me in, I will bow nervously and try to stammer out the words a wise friend of mine said: "Because You love me, You know You do."

Then I think I will add this: "I know Bill and Jim and Steve. They're over there in the front row. They're my friends."

I guess I've reached middle age.
My wife forced me to stay up till 12.

26

Doubting Dad

There lives more faith in honest doubt,
believe me, than in half the creeds.

ALFRED, LORD TENNYSON

෧෨

I'm sneakin' into heaven with a borrowed halo.

CHRIS RICE

We have a dog by the name of Mojo, which is a Bible name, of course. Named after Moses and Jonah (Moses who stuttered, and Jonah who ran away from home a lot), this Maltese–Shih Tzu lap dog does not appreciate my laptop computer. I was typing away one night when Mojo leaped onto my lap and somehow managed to push Control+Alt+Delete, a sequence that completely shut my computer down. I kid you not. The dog had no sense of remorse whatsoever, just sat there begging to be scratched, unaware that she might have erased the last hour of my life, and possibly some truly deep thoughts.

After Mom and Dad moved in, Mojo became Dad's number one fan, following him around their suite, pouncing on his lap whenever he sat down, grinning up at him past crooked teeth. The two sat by the window happily munching bananas, lost in a one-sided conversation.

Dad loved the old saying, "If you can start the day without caffeine, live without complaining, eat the same food every day and be grateful, relax without liquor, and sleep without the aid of drugs, you are probably the family dog."

"That dog is a blessing," Dad would say, and not just for the company but for what she was teaching him about doubt and fear.

He had been experiencing his share of both lately.

One night, in the midst of a short conversation, Dad asked, "Do you have any books on doubt?"

His words caught me by surprise. My father? Doubt? Are you kidding? I am young enough to have doubts, but not this rock-solid Christian who has loved and served God for almost seven decades. Preaching when called upon. Telling others the certainty of what Christ has done for him. How many times did he tell me that our faith is a fact, not a feeling? Perhaps there is more of Thomas than Peter in him, after all.

Dad seemed to notice my raised eyebrows, so he voiced the question again: "Do you have any books on doubt?"

"I think so," I said. "Uh…is it for a research project?"

"It's for me," he said, unashamed.

Ever since I can remember, Dad has turned to books for comfort and guidance. Our house was filled with them. They lined the hallways and bedrooms and counters and bathrooms. We weren't big on artwork, saving our money for bookshelves instead. Winter evenings were spent playing ice hockey and rarely concluded without the benediction of a good book.

Favorite books of my childhood are in my study now, their covers torn, the pages bent. After Dad's request, I ran my fingers along the shelves. *Tom Sawyer. Robinson Crusoe. Arabian Nights.* As a child I wished I could add pages to these books; they were always too short. The happy endings were like discovering a quarter in your piece of birthday cake, a bonus to an already breathtaking day.

Is my father wondering if a happy ending can be written into his story? After all, who pens a tale where the hero ends up old, forgetful, and forgotten, reliant on others for everything? For the majority, old age is the most difficult chapter, with Doubt and Fear playing the lead roles. We spend our lives writing our story but one day realize that no one gets out of life alive. That the only way out is the way of trust.

What shall I say to my father?

In Bible college I learned all the standard responses to doubt, but I've never encountered it in someone so near. Frederick Buechner calls doubt the "ants in the pants of faith." It's like the stinging nettle on our golf course. You go looking for your lost ball, and this pesky plant haunts you for the rest of the round, requiring that you spend more time scratching than slicing golf balls. But sometimes it's the nettle that assures you you're alive; that breeds stubborn determination to find answers, to press on.

In my study, I managed to locate two good books on the topic. Dad thanked me for them, but a few days later when the subject arose, he didn't mention the books. Instead, he gave me a verse he had hand-written on a piece of paper and was carrying in his pocket. A verse from Psalm 23:

> Surely goodness and mercy shall follow me all the days of my life:
> and I will dwell in the house of the LORD forever. (KJV)

One word was underlined: *surely*.

David did not say, "You know, it is quite likely that goodness and mercy may possibly, perhaps, probably, if I'm really lucky, follow me around for a week or two."

No, the verse speaks with assurance that God's goodness will provide, that His mercy will pardon. Forever.

Amid the unnerving changes in his life, Dad needed the promise of a changeless God. With the uncertainty of where he would live, he needed a reminder of his heavenly home. With his memory beginning to fail, he found comfort in meditating on the One "with whom there is never the slightest variation or shadow of inconsistency" (James 1:17, Phillips).

And God didn't just use that verse. He used the dog, too.

One June evening we were lounging on our covered deck, watching the sky change color in the west. Ragged edges of black appeared over the Rockies, growled a warning, and started their slow march toward us. Mojo was slumped on Grandpa's lap, but once the clouds rattled with thunder, she began to shake like she had one paw in a light socket.

"It'll be okay," Dad whispered, patting her Ewok head reassuringly. But she wouldn't be comforted. "I've got you, don't worry," he murmured, massaging her shoulders. But she wouldn't listen. An irrational fear had gripped her tiny body. She trembled. She shook. She panted. And as the clouds tumbled closer and the rain touched down, she leaped from his lap, darted under a wheelbarrow, and refused to come out.

"Come here, Moje," Dad beckoned, leaning forward. "Don't be silly. It's gonna be okay."

I couldn't resist saying something. "So do you think God feels a little like we do right now?" I thought of the bumblebees I kept in jars without lids when I was a child. "Trying to comfort poor dumb, frightened creatures who can't understand what's going on? Do you think He's trying to tell us to trust Him? That's it's all right?"

As Dad sat talking to the wheelbarrow, the storm ended and the dog emerged from her hiding place, creeping across the grass and back onto his lap. A smile lit up his face.

I know for a fact that the doubts lingered and the questions remained unanswered. But they seemed to fade into insignificance that night as he massaged Mojo's shoulders, perhaps thinking of a heavenly Father who holds us in His arms amid life's storms, whispering, "Don't be silly, My child. It's gonna be okay."

27

The Winding Road

Keep changing. When you're
through changing, you're through.

BRUCE FAIRCHILD BARTON

My mother, a homemaker and author, seamstress and personal chef for five, is taking her leave of this earth in a bedroom twenty feet from ours in the suite we built during easier times. Beyond her window lies the eastern sky, from which numerous preachers promised Christ would return one glad morning.

"I never thought I'd live to be this old," she whispers as I rub her feet—feet that are colder and smaller than I remember them. Dying people have no reason to be less than honest. And she insists she is dying, that she doesn't want to go on, that she simply won't stand for it.

"We were told the Rapture would happen during the war," she frowns. "Then they said we wouldn't live to have children. That the end of the world was near. That we'd never see the year 2000. Now I wonder what was true and what wasn't."

I smile and shake my head. I must have missed the Bible college class when they told us what to do when your aging mother embraces agnosticism. Mom was forever the woman of faith. Quick with a Bible verse. She was the one who brought Old Testament stories to life for me, soothing my insomnia with promises of God that I've clung to in some dark hours. And she spanked me. Yes, she certainly did. But her heart was never entirely in it. Her spankings were more like apologies. When she said it hurt her more than me, I believed her. And I loved her for it. I caress her hands now and wonder how they ever held the leather tightly enough to administer those timid doses. I grew up listening to these hands tickle the piano, while her soft voice sang hymns that still comfort me.

The last few months I've needed that comfort. With increasing frequency, Dad has been asking questions he has always known the answers for, and Mom has been concerned about him. A few days ago in the middle of the night, she fell, leaving dark bruises on her forehead and ribs. I don't know if she passed out, but somehow, despite the pain, she stubbornly managed to find her way through the laundry room and into our bedroom where she flipped on the light and announced that the end of the world was nigh. It was three in the morning, and it was like the angel Gabriel himself had opened the door, held a trumpet to his lips, and blasted a high C. After I ruled out the angel, I thought it was Dad playing one of his practical jokes, but there was nothing practical about it.

"She needs to take these, and she needs bed rest," a busy doctor told us a few hours later, his voice filled with optimism. "She should be fine." But as the days pass, we realize that she is far from fine. Her speech has slurred, her thoughts are jumbled. It may be the medication, but whatever it is, Mom has taken a bad turn, not knowing up from down.

And just like that, we are facing the fact that a chapter is ending, that both Mom and Dad need more care than we are capable of giving them. For a time, we hired a home-care nurse, but the folks now require twenty-four-hour care. We need to keep track of their medication, pay their bills, cook meals, and do the laundry.

Sometimes the door is left open in the night when the temperature is below freezing. Dad is confused much of the time. One morning he tapped on my study door, though it was already open. In his hand he held a blank check. "You fill it in," he said. "I'll pay whatever you want to stay here." I blinked and swallowed, wondering what to say.

My brothers and sister and I huddled together, seeking wise medical, financial, and spiritual counsel. We've prayed so many times that the ending would be easier than this, that we wouldn't have to pry the dog from Dad's lap and put him in a home. But I've also been praying each time I travel that the house would be standing when we return. That the stove and microwave and gas fireplace would be off.

One night I had quite an angry talk with God on my evening walk, informing Him of some things I was quite certain He had not thought of yet. It ended with me explaining that He couldn't possibly know what it was like to shoulder the responsibilities of having to care for an aging parent, and suddenly I was silenced by the realization that Jesus was no stranger to my situation.

What was He doing while in agony on the cross?

John, the "disciple Jesus loved," humbly tells us in chapter 19 of his gospel:

> When Jesus saw his mother standing there beside the disciple he loved, he said to her, "Woman, he is your son." And he said to this disciple, "She is your mother." And from then on this disciple took her into his home. (NLT)

As I rubbed Mom's feet, these thoughts swirled through my mind again. While in horrible agony, Jesus was thinking of, caring for, and honoring His mother.

Honoring our aging parents means not despising them for the "inconvenience" their age and fading health brings us. It means respecting their difficulties and shouldering their burdens. It means treasuring them and helping them and getting them a drink, as they did for us when we were whiny little kids. And sometimes it means putting them in the care of others.

One of the most difficult things I have ever done was take the car keys from Dad. Something inside me died that day. I took the dog from his lap and wished I could go somewhere and cry for about a week.

When I was twelve or thirteen I saw my parents wrestle through these same questions with my grandfather. In the end, I watched Dad carry his father's small suitcase to the car and drive Grandpa to his last earthly residence: a small seniors' home.

Today a chapter ends and a new one begins, as I find myself doing the same.

28

Great Escapes

*God does not comfort us to make
us comfortable, but to make us comforters.*

JOHN HENRY JOWETT

One reason a dog is such a comfort in tough times is that he doesn't say anything. Doesn't second-guess your decisions or write you notes questioning your sanity. And of course there are humans who will encourage you too. Some told us of their own journey, and we took comfort in the knowledge that we were not alone, that others had walked this path before—triumphing with humor and grace. Here are three of their stories.

∞

In 1967, William Crozier's dad walked out on his wife, his children, and the church he pastored. William didn't speak to his father for years. But after he married, he knew he must make things right.

"In the early nineties," writes William, "Dad was run over by a little old lady in a very big car and dragged one hundred feet. Since then he has lived with a brain injury, and I have tried to honor him. Dad and I go out to lunch often. He proposes to every woman in the restaurant on the way in, and on the way out introduces me as his pastor-son who will do the ceremony. We laugh. And people who understand laugh, too."

William and his wife rented an apartment for his dad in a nearby town, helping him live independently for as long as he could, and when an aunt of nearly eighty was hospitalized with a stroke, they were surprised by the joy they discovered in helping her too.

"She was coached to do exercises involving moving her lips repeatedly and making really rude noises, so that she could regain her speech," says William. "Her room happened to face the hallway where the elevator doors opened, so we challenged her to pucker up and make noises with great enthusiasm whenever the doors to the elevators opened. Innocent people exiting the elevator were greeted with smooching sounds and even some outstanding raspberries, made all the more hilarious by the fact that she seldom remembered to put her teeth in. How she loved gumming people into hysterics! In fact, it may be part of the reason for her quick recovery.

"More important than her sense of humor was her forgiveness of my father. She saw him at his worst forty years ago when he left and yet was so graceful to him. She wasn't just content to talk about forgiveness; she allowed him to live in it."

ꩦ

"When my parents entered the early stages of Alzheimer's," recalls Katherine Dutcher, "they failed to recognize that they were in desperate need of assisted-living arrangements. On weekends my siblings and I took turns being there for them. But for five days each week they were alone, and our concern for their safety grew with each visit.

"Hoping to convince them that they needed help, my brother Tom, a very good negotiator, explained home health-care aid and assisted living, showing them brochures and laying out the costs for the different options. Before he could finish, they became so upset he had to quit. Though Tom was the only one to say anything, Dad shook his finger at my sister and me, stating angrily, 'You girls are no good. You are trying to kick us out of our own house. Tom is the only good one. You two are out of the will.'

"After we left, my brother Tom teased us: 'You're out of the will and I'm not!'

"Since we wanted to respect their wishes to stay in their home, we decided to hire a home health-care aide. But things went from bad to worse. 'I've never been so disappointed in you,' Dad said, looking at me.

"I felt hopeless and guilty and afraid. Afraid they would hurt themselves or, worse yet, hurt someone else while driving. I began to realize we could not solve this problem ourselves. And so we began to pray.

"One morning at 2:30, the phone rang. It was one of Mom and Dad's neighbors. Thinking he had bought the neighbor's truck, Dad found the keys under the floor mat and drove the truck through two neighbors' yards, over a small tree, and into a ditch. The police were finally able to get him home and settled in for the night, and the gracious neighbor assured me he wasn't pressing charges.

"Frightened, I called Tom so he could be there by morning. But at 7 a.m. the neighbor called again. This time Dad thought he had bought the man's backhoe. Unable to get it started, he darted for home when the neighbor began yelling at him.

"Knowing they were in trouble, Mom and Dad packed a suitcase and were backing out of the driveway when the police arrived. The officer seized their car keys and their drivers' licenses, foiling their great escape.

"God answered our prayers in a surprising way. The day of Mom and Dad's attempted escape, Tom arrived to find that they couldn't wait to move out of that dreadful neighborhood. After all, they couldn't trust the neighbors.

"Within a month we had found an assisted living home near my sister's house. It came complete with a patio where Mom could feed the birds, and a view of a wooded area where Dad could watch the deer. At last they were safe and happy."

∽

Jackie Larson calls her father "the product of a poverty-stricken Depression-era home, self-educated and one of the smartest men I ever met." But lessons learned from his own abusive father and a weakness for drinking wrought destruction in his character. "He lived a self-centered life," writes Jackie. "Hardheaded, he could be a mean drunk, catastrophically unsuited to the task of stepfather to my half siblings. His only softening influences were his mother, his two daughters, and their children.

"Although he paid for me to attend a Christian school and college, he remained adamant that I not preach to him, and so I kept my mention of God to little cards and notes I sometimes sent him."

During her final visit with her father, Jackie played the piano and sang for the residents of the nursing home in which he now lived. It was Christmastime, and she played all the carols requested, as well as a few familiar and comforting hymns.

"Are there any final requests?" she asked.

Her father, a lifelong agnostic, frail in his wheelchair, but still vigorous of mind at eighty-three, looked straight at her and said, " 'The Old Rugged Cross.' "

Startled, she played the notes and began to sing:

On a hill far away stood an old rugged cross,
The emblem of suffering and shame;
And I love that old cross where the dearest and best
For a world of lost sinners was slain.

So I'll cherish the old rugged cross,
Till my trophies at last I lay down;
I will cling to the old rugged cross,
And exchange it some day for a crown.

"As I pushed him back to his room," Jackie remembers, "I couldn't help wondering what those words meant to him.

" 'Dad,' I said, 'I have a final request for you. For decades, you've told me you were agnostic. You've said, "Don't bother me with your religious views." But now that you've had some time to reflect on this, are you willing to consider trust in Christ? I believe we're all sinners and only Jesus can save us through His death on the cross. I believe that He's the only way we can be right with God and get to heaven, and that we need to accept that gift and trust in Him. Do you believe that, Dad?'

"He looked at me with steady blue eyes. 'More and more, kid,' he said. 'More and more.'

"Dad drifted off to sleep, and the moment ended. His condition worsened rapidly, and he died not long after our visit.

"I do not know for sure the condition of his soul. But I can't help thinking of the day I discovered—tucked safely away in his box of chess pieces—all the Christian cards and notes I ever wrote him. And I do know that Jesus came looking for lost sheep. Perhaps He found another one in that nursing home. Perhaps this tired old lamb, weary of a life lived without communion with the Great Shepherd, approached heaven's gate with a final request and was welcomed home."

29

Freedom 82

*The worst thing in your life may contain seeds
of the best. When you can see crisis as an opportunity,
your life becomes not easier, but more satisfying.*

JOE KOGEL

For his eighty-second birthday I gave my father a rather expensive maple pool cue. The irony of the gift was not lost on any of us.

Back in the 1930s, Ying's Pool Hall was the favorite hangout for teenagers in the riverside hamlet of Elora, Ontario, Canada. There my dad learned to smoke, drink, swear, chew, and hit a spittoon. Cold winter nights of my childhood were warmed by his stories of those days. Of winning a few bucks betting on billiards. Of cheating the blind owner out of small change.

One dark and memorable Halloween, Dad and a few cronies moved the pool hall outhouse back a few feet—much to the surprise of some dear inebriated soul and drawing the attention of the local constable. When he told me this story, my admiration grew as wide as my smile. Through the years I've attempted a little mischief myself, but I'm sorry to report that I never truly mastered it as Dad did.

Twenty-one years before I was born, God put an arm around my father and refused to let go. "I sipped my last beer and took a final drag from a cigarette," he liked to say. "I threw the pack into the fireplace and slammed the door on the pool hall, never to return."

One summer night at a hot-dog roast, Dad first set eyes on a shy brunette by the name of Bernice. She would become my mother, but as far as I know it was not something they discussed that evening. Instead, they sat and watched the clouds gather, knowing that Adolf Hitler was ransacking Europe, that Dad would soon join the troops and set out to chase him home.

Dad never did find Adolf, but he chased down my mother, and after the Allied victory parade, the two climbed aboard a train bound for western Canada to study for the ministry.

After poring over books of theology for several winters, he was ordained by the Evangelical Free Church. Following several brief forays with small congregations, he returned to the Bible school where he had studied and joined its staff. The regulations were strict there. Your hair could not touch your ears (unless you were a girl), and sleeves must end below the elbows (unless you were a boy). There were clear guidelines for abstaining from Sunday afternoon football, playing pool, listening to rock music, smoking, drinking, chewing, and the purchasing of spittoons.

I loved my childhood. Mischief was never far away. You didn't need to steal a car or graffiti a building to get the attention of grownups. Winking at your girlfriend would do the trick.

Though Dad didn't always agree with the rules, he was careful to keep one of them. When we visited friends with pool tables, Dad stood off to one side, enjoying the smiles on our faces as we played, but never picking a cue up himself. For him it characterized his old life, and he wanted no part of it. "You play pool, you play the fool," he sometimes said.

When he and Mom moved into the Golden Hills Lodge, peers begged him to join in their pool games, which went on most evenings until someone fell asleep—sometimes on the table.

Dad told them he hadn't picked up a cue in about sixty years. They couldn't believe it. They stopped asking, perhaps reasoning that anyone this rusty wouldn't be much fun to beat anyway.

One night while I sat eating from a candy dish he kept well stocked for the grandkids, Dad confided in me that he still experienced an uneasy feeling about the game. I asked him if they were placing wagers or cheating each other. He didn't think so. I told him we could baptize the pool table, get it saved. He laughed.

And so it was that I presented him with his birthday gift and watched his face light up like he had just received a bike for his sixth birthday. "It's left-handed, like you," I said. That just added to his excitement.

Next thing I knew he was lining up shots and mowing down surprised opponents. And he was smoking again. And swearing. And drinking beer like a fish. I'm kidding. But the old guy was good.

At the age of eighty-two he would bend over that table, sight in the eightball, and take it down hard. Dad couldn't remember his name sometimes, but he could play pool. My sons and I tried to beat him. We seldom succeeded. The years had been kind to his aim, and he smiled as he played. It was one thing he could do well, one card he could still play.

Dad smiled about other things too. For the most part, he enjoyed his new surroundings not far from our house. Some of the residents were friends he hadn't talked to in years. I noticed as the days turned into months that he was afforded a more noticeable gentleness, and I'm convinced that it was grace once again. I guess God's grace is there whatever the season; it has no expiration date, no statute of limitations.

Soon, however, Dad's health and memory deteriorated further. A nurse sat me down to explain why we would have to move my parents to the long-term-care wing of a hospital. As she talked, the most amazing thing happened. She began to cry. "I'll miss him," she said. "He's been so kind."

If there is any blessing in Alzheimer's, perhaps it is this: Sometimes you're a little confused by the sorrow of others. Your children drive you to your new home a little farther away, and you point out the window at wheat fields and cows and elephants in the clouds, wondering why your child doesn't share your enthusiasm during this Sunday afternoon drive on a Wednesday. You've got a pool cue in the backseat. It's a great day to be alive.

30

Caregiving 101

Dying is a very dull, dreary affair,
and my advice to you is to have nothing to do with it.
W. SOMERSET MAUGHAM

D uring this time I began to receive invitations to speak at conferences for health-care providers at hospitals and nursing homes. I eagerly accepted, and I'm sure it had nothing to do with the fact that some were government-subsidized conferences and offered more than an honorarium of mileage and a T-shirt. I counted it an honor and found these unheralded servants ripe for laughter. I also found them exhausted. One lady told me, "I'm so tired I fall into bed at night and I don't have the energy to use the Clapper." And so I tell them of the message a friend of mine has on his answering machine:

Hello, and welcome to the Mental Health Hotline. If you are obsessive-compulsive, please press 1 immediately. If you are co-dependent, please ask someone else to press 2. If you have multiple personalities, please press 3, 4, 5, and 6. If you are paranoid, we know who you are and what you want. Just stay on the line so we can trace the call. If you are depressed, it doesn't matter which number you push. No one will answer.

The health-care professionals laugh quite heartily at this, and then I tell them the sad reality—that this is the kind of answer many people receive when they're in need. But how I thank God that no one gets that kind of answer from them, that they walk in when others walk out.

They seem to like this, so I keep going. I tell them of the battles I've faced steering a family through Huntington's disease and epilepsy and a few other icebergs. And I tell them some of the things I've learned that have kept me relatively sane and well adjusted when life threatens to poke holes in my hull:

Laugh a little each day. Before I was born, my dad worked in a psychiatric ward in Quebec, Canada. I don't remember much about it, but Mom claims he would come home at night and describe some of the sad events of the day, often interspersing his dialogue with a good belly laugh. She couldn't believe it at first, but it was his way of finding the pulse of sanity in a dark place.

I find myself doing the same now in caring for my father. One summer day while I was visiting the hospital, a lady who serves as part-time chaplain pulled me aside. Her forehead was scrunched up, and I wondered what awful thing my father had done or said. "You told me he had been faithful to your mother for sixty years," she said, still scrunching. "Today he was watching TV and holding hands with a complete stranger." Of course I laughed. So did she. Sure, we cry and we pray, but sometimes laughter is our most effective weapon—perhaps the only one we have. And it sure beats oat bran.

Find a confidant. Miles Franklin said, "Someone to tell it to is one of the fundamental needs of human beings." You don't need to give everyone you meet an organ recital, but who can put a price tag on the value of sharing his story, thoughts, feelings, and sometimes tears with a trusted other?

Some communities have caregiver support groups. If you can't find one, start one. If you can't start one, get a pet. Sometimes my dog is my support group. She's the only one who will listen without interrupting. It's like the old Swedish proverb: "Shared joy is a double joy; shared sorrow is half a sorrow."

Carve hurry from your life. I wish someone had informed me earlier that there is nothing noble about a nervous breakdown and nothing selfish about taking care of your own needs. When I discovered that "no" is a complete sentence, I freed time for pursuing my gifts. When I learned to enjoy things without owning them, I forgot about the Joneses. When I began hanging out with positive people, I topped off my energy tank. When I began taking care of myself, I found I was better equipped to take good care of others. Stillness is rejuvenating. Sometimes the most pressing thing you can possibly do is take a complete rest.

Exercise three times a week. Bodily exercise profits a little. Of course, it didn't help my mother. She started walking a mile a day when she was sixty. She's eighty-three now and we don't know where she is.

Enjoy the right food and take longer to eat it. My philosophy on eating is the same as Miss Piggy's: Never eat more than you can lift. But middle age informs me that my philosophy is flawed. Pants that fit last Thursday are malfunctioning. So I need to acquaint myself with salmon, tomatoes, broccoli, nuts, and blueberries. And never pass up an opportunity to savor dessert. A recent study conducted by the dark chocolate industry indicates that dark chocolate is good for you.

Run away from home. Find a way to get away. If the budget is low, develop a great imagination. Close your eyes and imagine that your bath is at a spa in the Himalayas—without the monkeys. Never just listen to your favorite music. Pretend you're at a concert, or giving one. When you can't take what you've been taking any longer, take a vacation.

Take care of the home front. Who we are and what we are able to accomplish come directly from the foundations we build. So work on your relationships inside your tightest circles. Those of us who care for aging parents must not forget our own children.

Worry less. Worry steals everything worthwhile from today and adds nothing worthwhile to tomorrow. Worried people see problems; concerned people find solutions.

Remember you're more amazing than you think. In a selfish age, those who care for others make God smile. So never underestimate the power of a kind word, a touch, a smile, a tear, or a compliment. You are the answer to someone's prayer. Be assured that there will be resistance, but the rewards are out of this world.

Go looking for the blessings. Don't worry, you'll find them. They're everywhere.

31

My Shark Hunter

We are here to add what we can to,
not to get what we can from, life.
Sir William Osler

Ever since he was knee-high to a Doberman, the boy was fearless. Take him to the ocean and he'd jump in looking for sharks. Take him to the mountains and he'd see how high he could climb. One day when he was five, I watched in horror as he jumped off a roof, a garbage bag duct-taped to his back. It didn't go well for him. So we set the bone, and he tried it again.

We couldn't be more opposite, my son and I. The higher he climbs, the more he believes God is with him. Not me. I believe God put us on dry land and said, "*Lo,* I am with you always."

In his first year of Bible college, Steve called one night to ask me for money. "I'm sorry," I said. "You have reached this number in error. Please hang up and call your Uncle Dan."

"I scaled a three-hundred-foot cliff today," he said, undaunted. "You'd have loved it."

Right. His father, who contracts vertigo standing on a skateboard.

For years I've wondered what God would make of our son. Would He call him to be a crash-test dummy? A professional bungee jumper? Or would he fulfill every North American parent's dream by settling down in a huge house with a nice wife and provide us some grandchildren to spoil?

The unexpected answer arrived by e-mail one day.

Dear Dad and Mom,

I just want you to know that I met a couple of nice girls and we're planning on being married. In Utah. Not really. But I did meet Lucy. You'll like her a lot. It's surprising how quickly you can find a justice of the peace down here. Lucy owns a tattoo parlor but seldom works. Her father won some money in a lottery, so she's set for life. I won't need to work anymore either. I've bought a Mercedes convertible and you'll be happy to know I put a chrome fish on the bumper.

If you haven't fainted yet, here's the truth. It may be more shocking. In the country of Uganda, the Lord's Resistance Army is committing atrocities against children that are too awful for me to put in this letter. Over the years they've abducted fifty thousand kids and turned the ones they haven't murdered into soldiers. I'd like to work with street children in Kampala. I'll be living with local missionaries. It will mean lots of needles and I'll need to raise a little money too.

Dad, I once heard you say that Jesus came to comfort us, not to make us comfortable. I guess I've been comforted enough; it's time to offer some to others.

Love from far away,

Your son, Steve

"Where do you think we went wrong?" I asked his mother. "Couldn't he just have a beach ministry in Hawaii?"

"It's what we've prayed for all these years," she said with a grin, "that he would live life on purpose."

"I think we blew it by having all those missionaries over for dinner or taking him to other countries and showing him what the real world looks like."

And so we found ourselves hugging our firstborn son good-bye as he embarked on a grand adventure half a world away. I hugged him until his ribs squeaked. One of us wiped tears. I won't tell you who.

It's funny, the questions people ask when they hear our son is in Uganda. This is the one I've heard a few dozen times: "Aren't you worried about his safety?" I'd be a fool not to admit that I have my moments. Check out a list of the most dangerous spots on earth, and Uganda is near the top. But is safety what we're here for? Isn't Complacency the most dangerous place on earth? Isn't Suburbia sucking the life out of more of our teenagers than any foreign country ever could?

I sat with a missionary the other day who is pouring her life out in Pakistan, patching bodies and souls for Jesus. She said she's the only missionary in her area whose parents support her being there.

I must be honest. I understand. There are times I'd rather Steve was home making good money—putting it away for my nursing-home bills. Yet I cannot hope for more than this: that my children will hear God's voice despite a noisy culture, and that they will obey.

A few nights before Steve left, I asked him what he'd miss most about home. "The dog," he said, smiling.

Then why is it that I found him studying family photos and lounging on the sofa watching an old Disney movie with his brother and sister? Was he killing time? Or saying good-bye to the remnants of childhood?

Whatever happened to the boy I used to build Lego-block villages with? The boy I taught to whistle and ride a bike? The boy who once put Kool-Aid in our shower head?

I've shed a few tears for sure. But mostly I've been smiling and giving thanks. For God's grace in giving me a son who's an updated and improved version of his father. For e-mail and cheap overseas phone rates.

And I'm thankful there are no sharks in Uganda.

32

Bumper Cars and Harpoons

When it comes to staying young,
a mind-lift beats a face-lift any day.

MARTY BUCELLA

∞

I still find each day too short for all the thoughts
I want to think, all the walks I want to take, all the books
I want to read, and all the friends I want to see.

JOHN BURROUGHS

I've been hanging out in nursing homes a little earlier than planned, and I've discovered that some of the inmates have managed to age gracefully, like gold-medal figure skaters. They are gliding through the golden years, smiling sweetly, bringing joy to others.

Then there are those who are determined to seek vengeance by using their wheelchairs as bumper cars and their canes as harpoons. When the grandkids visit, they spend the time whining about how the grandkids never visit. For them the glass is not just half empty; it's cracked and chipped, and the lemonade is sour. To say they are lacking fashion sense is like saying the Pacific is wet. The men wear black knee socks and wing-tipped white shoes. They only use two buttons on their shirt. The ladies wear dresses they bought from the tent and awning company and have their hair dyed neon blue.

My grandfather Callaway was a combination of the graceful and the geezer. He loved a good laugh, but he also loved to talk about his ailments once the entire family had gathered around the dinner table and the food had been doled out. Then suddenly, it was organ-recital time: "So I remember when the doctors had to root through me and take out my spleen. Stayed awake for the whole thing. Watched 'em dig it outta there all wrinkled and green. I asked 'em to pickle it for me. Put it in a jar. I kept it for years on the counter. Looked like a big hairy cucumber. Hey, where's everybody going? Mind if I eat your carrots?"

Grandpa gained a lot of weight in those days, and we saved money on groceries.

I loved and admired my grandfather immensely. He gave me money whenever I visited him, and though God had delivered him from alcoholism, he was the only man I've ever met who bought cough syrup in bulk, drinking it straight from the bottle.

I once enjoyed an evening with a seventy-five-year-old by the name of Donald Cole. Mr. Cole travels the country speaking at conferences and hosts a radio show during which he dispenses spiritual advice to callers, grownups and five-year-olds alike. During our conversation, Mr. Cole mentioned to me that he runs several miles a day, which caught me off guard—like having a guy in a Smart Car pull up to a stoplight beside you, glance your way, and rev his engine.

I got to thinking about how nice it would be to jog when I turn seventy-five. Maybe it's something my wife and I could do together. She could drive me out of town and drop me off—it would give purpose to my running. So I said something dumb to Mr. Cole, which is not something that took me entirely by surprise, because I seem to bounce between not opening my mouth wide when I should and opening it far too wide when I shouldn't. I said, "Boy, I'd sure like to be running like that when I'm your age."

He said, "Are you running now?"

I coughed slightly. I said, "I…ahem…came in third in a relay once."

He said, "If you aren't running now, you won't be then."

In other words, if I sit around eating lard-filled doughnuts in my thirties, when I turn sixty-five, my chances of waddling much farther than the refrigerator aren't great.

And it hit me that all of us are in training for the days to come. That if we are impatient, unkind, and unforgiving, we won't wake up at sixty-five to discover that people want to be around us. This made me wonder: *What kind of an old guy will I be?* And how do I live so my kids will want to visit me in the nursing home? By then, as the old saying goes, I will have silver in my hair, gold in my teeth, lead in my feet, and lots of natural gas, but I won't be wealthy without friends.

The older people I admire are those who have exercised the right creases on their face. Not the ones of petulance and complaint, but the ones turned upward on either side of their eyes. They live life on purpose. I fear that if some of us wrote down a mission statement it would look something like this:

> I will consider myself a success when I'm rich enough to do nothing but travel and eat and collect sea shells; when I can have it the way I want it; when the jerks around here start leaving me alone. I will consider myself a success when my wife wakes up to the fact that I'm marvelous, when I've got a big-screen TV and nothing but time on my hands to watch it.

Contrast this with the attitude of my friend Dave Epp. Dave visits the hospital a few times a week, and Mom and Dad are always glad to see him. After mourning the loss of his wife to cancer, Dave decided to use his pain, becoming a hospital chaplain, visiting those who can't get out, encouraging them with the love of Jesus, joking with them, and praying for them. Dave could wallow in bitterness, but he lives life on purpose, with significance.

The older people I admire still have their sense of humor intact. Anne Lamott calls laughter "carbonated holiness." Gerald Wheatley is so full of the stuff that you can almost hear him fizz. Last Sunday he greeted me in our church foyer with a new joke from the corny patch. "Did you hear about the guy who walks into a bar and asks, 'Does anyone here own that Rottweiler outside?' "

I hadn't heard about the guy, but I knew I was about to.

"A biker stands up, says, 'Yeah, that's my dog. What about it?'

" 'I think my Chihuahua killed him.'

"The biker laughs. '*What?* How could your little runt kill my Rottweiler?'

" 'Got stuck in his throat.' "

When you walk past a room and hear laughter, you want to find out what's causing it.

Few things give us more hope than a seventy-five-year-old who is reading good books, learning new truths, and discussing things besides the weather. She smiles more than she has reason to, laughs when she probably shouldn't, and talks to children and babies and pets.

I wrote down a few more things I admire in older people. It came out as a little poem, and I showed it to my mother. She smiled her approval, then gave me the kind of look that says, *You're young. One day you'll understand that it isn't all easy.* Still, I pinned it to the bulletin board so she could show it to her friends. Here it is:

You are not old.

Until you stop making new friends.

Until you start fighting change.

You are not old.

Until your past is bigger than your future.

Until you think the bad old days were all good.

Until you talk more of ills, spills, bills, and wills.

Than thrills.

Until you begrudge the spotlight

turned on a younger generation.

And stop shining it on them yourself.

You are not old as long as you can pray.

As long as you have the inner strength to ask:

How can I spread hope around?

How can I get the most out of the years I have left?

How can I make others homesick for heaven?

You are young at heart.

Until you decide you aren't.

I am happy to report that the little poem is still there, still pinned to the bulletin board. So far no one has harpooned it with a cane.

I used to be nostalgic, but now I can't remember anything.

33 Regrets, I Have a Few

Regret for time wasted can become a power for good in the time that remains, if we will only stop the waste and the idle, useless regretting.

ARTHUR BRISBANE

ᏬᏬ

My one regret in life is that I am not someone else.

WOODY ALLEN

When our children were barely done toddling, we had an agreement that any of them at any moment could go limp like a noodle when they passed within a foot of me. It was my job, of course, to catch them before they crashed to the floor, or the sidewalk, or into the pool. This was great fun for all of us. Apparently, however, they thought this agreement lasted for life, because although two of them have reached my height and are closing in on my weight, they still play Noodle, which is a big bundle of laughs for everyone but me.

As I write, I regret inventing that game.

I have strained muscles in both calves, and my lower back is throbbing. Thankfully, laughter eases my pain. And I am glad we've done our share of it. But man oh man, I think I may have pulled some fat in my left arm.

If we're honest, most of us have regrets. And chances are, they're larger than some silly game we invented.

I mentioned to Mom one night that I wished I had handled their aging better. She seemed startled. I confessed that I hadn't always known what to do. She took my hand and spoke these wonderful words: "How could you?"

Erma Bombeck called guilt "the gift that keeps on giving." Surely there is no other occupation so guilt-ridden as parenting, with the possible exception of raising your own parents. Some of our parents have worked for decades as travel agents for guilt trips. We long for the days before the invention of the telephone when parents could not dial our number to nag, "It's Mother's Day. You're the only one of the children who hasn't called yet. Are you okay? Did you fall down a well?"

Recently, I received a hand-scrawled note:

Dear Phil,

    You talk about your parents with such warmth. I wish I could. Mine lived a short drive up the Interstate, but I never visited them. I was too busy, too stressed, and too selfish. Now I guess it's too late.

    SP

I wish SP had left her name and address because there is something I'm itching to tell her.

There is not an honest one among us who won't admit to falling short. I have not walked in your shoes, but I've walked in mine, and they pinch a good deal of the time. We are—all of us—flawed creatures who make mistakes. Those who don't look like it are usually just craftier hypocrites. We live in a broken, fallen place among broken, fallen people. There is not a family that isn't dysfunctional, not a one of us that doesn't need forgiveness. Furthermore, there is not a shred of hope apart from the goodness of God, His grace, and the restoration He promises and provides.

Syndicated columnist Sydney J. Harris wisely wrote, "Regret for the things we did can be tempered by time; it is regret for the things we did not do that is inconsolable."[17]

Oh I know that regret is 96 percent useless. Wallow in it, and life is yours to miss, they say. And they're right. Regret is painful and paralyzing—like shooting yourself with a tranquilizer dart right before the big game. But we can learn from the regrets of others. I asked a few thousand people about regret. Seventy-six percent admitted to having their share. Here is a sampling of their honest responses:

- "I regret wasting money playing the lottery."
- "I regret marrying because I was lonely."
- "I'd like to have played more golf."
- "I wish I'd been more patient with my children and my parents."
- "I regret not telling others of Jesus when I had the chance."
- "That I didn't take time for my daughter. I was too busy with housework."
- "I regret that I'm not close to my dad. My parents divorced when I was five. All those years I saw him every other weekend."
- "Building a house that is far too big."
- "Not listening to my father and marrying someone who had no relationship with God."
- "Drifting apart from my wife after we lost a son."
- "I regret being so involved in committees at our church that I may have shown my kids I loved the committees more

than them. I wonder if that's partly why they don't attend
church now."

   ☉ "That I didn't learn of Jesus Christ sooner."

I must be honest and admit that I have a few regrets too. Let me put
them this way.

If I Could Raise My Kids Again

If I could raise my kids again I wouldn't be so uptight this time.
   I'd let them jump on beds in hotels.
   And pick the cat up by the tail.
      That way they'd figure out a little sooner
         How life works.

If I could raise my kids again I'd be a little goofier this time.
   I'd stand on the chair in our kitchen,
   And play the harmonica with my nose.
      I'd play more jokes on them too.
         Ones that involve expired milk.

If I could raise my kids again I'd ask more questions and listen
   to the answers.
   I'd teach them to give by giving, to love by loving.
   They'd see me on my knees
      Praying more often.
         Not just looking for the remote control.

If I could raise my kids again I'd play hooky from work
   sometimes.
   I wouldn't sign up for the rat race.

I'd enjoy things without owning them.
I'd buy a bigger library.
And a smaller television.

If I could raise my kids again I'd relax a little more.
I'd cut spankings by about 50 percent.
In number. In length. In enthusiasm.
I'd place more importance on good character than good grades.
I'd prepare them for life by letting them argue.
By letting them fail.

As it is, I'm glad I talked to them early about God.
About money.
About sex.
I'm glad I spent way too much money on vacations,
Necked in the living room with their mother,
And took them to church.

But if I could raise my kids again, I think I'd be better at it
this time.
I wouldn't care so much about clean walls or clean feet.
I wouldn't celebrate nice grass, I'd celebrate grass stains.
I'd tuck my children into bed each night
Without checking my watch.

The doctor tells me that it's not about to happen.
That I'm halfway to ninety.
That we won't be having children anytime soon.
So I guess I'll get to practice these things
On my grandchildren.

34

Dying Young

*My doctor gave me six months to live, but when
I couldn't pay the bill he gave me six months more.*

WALTER MATTHAU

☙❧

*You have to live every day as if it's your last,
because one of these days, you're bound to be right.*

BREAKER MORANT

There are times after I spend an evening in the nursing home when I get thinking to myself: *I don't want to get old. For one thing, if I stay in peak physical condition, I will be a drain on the medical system.* And so I have uncovered three ways to ensure that none of us ripens to an old age. I trust these will be of help to you.

1. Change your diet and exercise habits. I exercised for the last time today. Retired my sneakers. My dumbbells. My pass to the exercise room. The resolve began when an acquaintance of mine dropped dead of a heart attack yesterday. I did not know him well, but when I thought of the last time I saw him alive, how he was waddling toward the Twinkies in the supermarket, it hit me like a runaway grocery cart: *die eating.*

One of the things I love about the Bible is that it's full of food. You can hardly read a chapter where someone isn't eating or drinking or celebrating or chewing on some fruit.

And so tonight we will order out for pizza. And Chinese food. Right after the Meals on Wheels people leave.

Tomorrow I start the new exercise program. Beating around the bush. Jumping to conclusions. Dragging my heels. Pushing my luck. Building mountains out of molehills.

Besides, if God had wanted us to lift weights, He'd have made our arms heavier. And if you're worried about your looks, there's no need to. Sure, you may develop flabby thighs, but your stomach will cover them.

2. Have more children: Children are messy, and they won't let you sleep a wink. Having children is like installing a NASCAR track in your head. It's noisy. Besides, the average male child costs roughly $3.4 million (that's in Legos alone) by the time he is eight, and you can double that if you have a darling little girl who steals your heart. Oh sure, they start out cuddly and they giggle, but don't be fooled. They are here with one thing in mind: getting you off the planet.

Grownups have always been suspicious of children. I realized this when I was very small and could tell that they were trying to get rid of me. They told us smoking was bad for us, knowing that if they said this we'd try it out and maybe get hooked for life—or death. They covered my crib with lead-based paints. There were no childproof lids on the aspirin bottle, no seat belts, air bags, or guardrails. They encouraged us to ride in the back of pickups or build our own go-carts and parachutes. We ate worms and mud pies. We played with BB guns and smashed rocks with a hammer and no goggles. They never offered us bike helmets or bottled water, and they introduced us to things like monkey bars.

I was just a wee little kid when grownups encouraged me to play ice hockey. They strapped blades on my feet, handed me a sharp stick and something called a puck. They pushed me out on the ice, then stood behind plywood sheets and wire mesh to see what happened. When we started having too much fun, they'd yell, "Kill him! Kill him!" I knew what they wanted. They wanted me dead. They knew I was a threat to a long and peaceful life.

So have more children. It's not too late. If you're a little older, think of Sarah and Abraham. Or of Satyabhama Mahapatra of India, a sixty-five-year-old retired schoolteacher who recently gave birth to a baby boy to become the world's oldest mother. Satyabhama and her husband have been married fifty years, but this is their first child.[18]

3. Travel to exotic places. I recommend a honeymoon in Iraq or cycling from Beirut to Jerusalem. Pack light. Carry explosives.

Okay, I've been joking and hoping all the while that you wouldn't write me a letter before you reach the conclusion.

The truth is, I've needed to laugh lately.

My father's mind and body are worsening fast, and when I visit, he asks me to read the psalms to him. As I do, one word keeps surfacing: *remember*. Depressed and lonely, David finds comfort in remembering:

- God's faithfulness
- God's goodness
- God's mercy
- God's justice
- God's miracles
- God's compassion
- God's blessing
- God's leading
- God's protection
- God's deliverance

And as I read these wonderful truths, I am struck by a terrible irony: I am reading commands about remembering to a man who can't remember my name. It's hard not to reflect on the fact that if this thing is remotely hereditary, I'm in trouble. There's something about Alzheimer's that makes me think I have a license to nurse my anger, to fertilize and water it, to trim back the dead stuff, so the plant has lots of light. Yet that was never my father's way. As proof, he smiles at me as I read, and I hope I'll do the same for my kids, should my turn ever come.

After visiting my parents one night, I came home to the sound of the phone ringing. A voice said, "Mr. Callaway, I don't much like your sense of humor. What does laughing have to do with being a Christian? We're in the last days here, and this is hardly a time for laughter."

I said, "Is that you, Dad?"

The caller didn't find that funny.

I wish I'd thought to tell him that if I don't laugh, the wheels will fall off. That if I can't laugh, I'm one more sad example of how evil sometimes wins. But I did manage to say, "I have so much to rejoice about. I've been forgiven. Eternity is waiting. I get a little excited about that."

Now that I've had time to think about it, I'd also add that I hope the caller wakes before he dies. That I want to die young…as old as I can.

You see, I think we stay young by keeping our eyes in the right places. By not wasting time placing discouraging phone calls. Or listening to gossip. By inviting friends over to dinner even if the carpet is stained and the sofa faded. By eating ice cream nine times a week.

I think we stay young by centering our thoughts on things that are pure, lovely, and of good report. By putting our arms out car windows more often. By burning expensive candles before they melt in storage.

By getting so excited about the love of Jesus that our teeth can barely keep up with our mouth.

So tomorrow morning I think I'll pull out those sneakers and the dumbbells and the alfalfa sprouts.

You'll be happy to know that, unlike Satyabhama, we've decided against having more children anytime soon. At least until we find a nursing home with a kindergarten attached.

Tom livens up the nursing home with another Bee Gees flashback.

35

The Move to Nunavut

God gave us memories that
we might have roses in December.
SIR JAMES M. BARRIE

O ur children have reached the age where they are moving out one by one, sometimes closing the door, and often returning to raid the fridge. It couldn't happen fast enough for me. The latest to go is our daughter, Rachael, who stole my heart eighteen years ago. She is graduating from a Christian high school with plans to move on, to study in England, then travel the world. She has been threatening to leave since third grade, and it couldn't come fast enough for me.

She has been eating our food, driving our car, and keeping us up late most nights. Years ago she left her initials on our dryer and carved OINK! into the arm of my old rocking chair. I noticed it while I was snacking late one night.

Rachael has bleached her bedroom carpet with nail polish remover. And painted her walls a shade of pink that causes me to cringe.

I promised her once that the moment she graduated, her furniture would be out on the front lawn. The door would be locked, the keys changed. We'll have sold the place and moved to Nunavut, where the real estate is cheap.

She laughed. "Oh Dad," she said. It's a phrase she's used a lot through the years.

During the graduation ceremony, Rachael took center stage to deliver the valedictory address. It was the first time in world history a Callaway had experienced such an honor. I ain't sure why. I thunk the rest of us would have did goodly.

"Our class is going to do amazing things," she began, throwing half a smile my way. "We are going to be rich. Famous. We are going to turn this world upside down with our impeccable charm and our fashion sense. Yes, we are going to be sports stars, movie stars, and pop stars. We are going to be scholars and musicians and politicians."

Thankfully she wasn't finished.

"When I was a little girl," she continued, "these are the things I thought characterized graduates. Maybe it was all those Disney movies we watched. Happily ever after. Wish upon a star. Dream, dream, dream. But I'm starting to find out those dreams were too small.

"Our motto is 'To the Ends of the Earth.' Maybe we chose it because our little town seems like the end of the world. Or maybe it's because our dream is to stand out from the crowd. To serve Jesus wherever we are. I've been reading of missionaries who packed their belongings in a coffin when they left home, fully expecting never to return. Some of us may go to Africa or China and never come back. Others will end up in Moose Jaw, or Seattle, or Cuba. It's my prayer that we'll serve Him wherever we are."

I was sitting near the front, hoping she wouldn't look my way and see my misty eyes. Was this the little girl I carried and cuddled and loved? All grown up and a preacher too? How could a troubled kid like me grow up to deserve the joy of seeing his daughter follow Jesus? And where did the years go? She's barely out of her high chair. Last week she was showing us her finger paintings. This week she'll show us her diploma.

"Those whose goal is to be famous and own lots of stuff are headed for disappointment whether they get it or not," she is saying. "All around us people are living for themselves. I would like to present to you the rest. This class is going to do amazing things. We are going to be poor, we are going to be ridiculed, mocked, and persecuted. But we will turn this world upside down with the love of God, because His strength is made perfect in weakness."

That evening more than a hundred people visited our house to celebrate and thank her for her speech. A few were complete strangers who heard there was free food. And after the last one left, I told Ramona of the glorious freedom we would experience when all our children are gone. Of the financial savings. After all, we had to remortgage the house to pay for Rachael's prom dress. We can enjoy lunch on our own schedule. Dinner, too. We can watch movies that are not in the New Release section. We can take out our hearing aids and play our music loud. Old hymns at deafening levels. No one will burst into the room scowling at us. We can go to bed at 10 p.m. and rest in peace. We can chase each other through the house wearing whatever we please.

Then why the tears as we stood looking at Rachael's empty room? The Winnie-the-Pooh border. The carpet scarred by nail polish remover. Because there are times I'd gladly trade every carpet in the house for another evening when she sat on my lap begging for one more story, one more piggyback ride, one more hug good night.

Yet our house is far from empty. In every room you'll find memory marks. In the kitchen, an oak cabinet bears a black scar where the candles on a surprise birthday cake almost brought the house down. We smile when we look at it. Sit in the living room and you can almost smell the popcorn from those nights we popped it onto a clean sheet on the floor. Dig deeply enough and you'll find old kernels buried in the sofa. Ah, memories.

And so we give thanks to God for what we have. For the wisdom to make memories over making money. To hold these children close while we could. And we're thankful we have one more child left at home. Sometimes I hear him and his friends lugging guitars and drums and heavy amplifiers down the stairs, carving more memory marks in the walls.

"Oops," they say.

I'm thankful I'm still young enough to sneak downstairs and pull the main breaker.

36

The Slow Good-Bye

When I hear somebody sigh, "Life is hard,"
I am always tempted to say, "Compared to what?"
SYDNEY J. HARRIS

Comedy was not my first choice. I wanted to be strong and good-looking. I wanted to have girls talk about me in front of my back. But I discovered early in life that the gals weren't looking for a sense of humor. They wanted solid chiseled features. And money for snacks. I had neither. So my dad tried to console me: "Poverty is hereditary," he said. "You get it from your children."

A sense of humor is too. I got it from my dad.

For the most part, comedians come from either of two backgrounds: severely depressed or extremely happy. Trust me on this, there is seldom middle ground. I grew up in a family where laughter was a staple. Where my parents loved each other and loved their children. My earliest memories are of Mom reading me *Winnie-the-Pooh* and Dad hiding in darkened rooms waiting to scare the living daylights out of me. Each of our three children has at some point experienced me pulling back their collars and sneezing down their necks. I got the idea from my dad. (I highly recommend it as a family tradition. I guarantee it's something your child will remember for years. Before you sneeze, though, make sure it's your child.)

The older I get, the more this sense of humor is coming in handy.

Mom and Dad lie in separate beds in the same hospital now, not quite knowing where they are. Each time I visit, they ask me about it, so I explain it to them like it's the first time, and the lights come on, then quickly fade.

I once asked my dad the secret to their lengthy marriage, and his eyes twinkled. "Senility," he said. "I wake up beside her each morning and I can't remember who she is. So each day is a new adventure."

It was funny back then.

But now the two old lovers are saying a slow good-bye to this earth, surrounded by children who love them and nurses whose sweetness surprises me at times.

Looking for Dad the other night, I found him slumped in a chair, tears streaming down his cheeks. "It's all right," said a slender young nurse, placing a gentle arm about his shoulder.

"Hey," I joked to her, "he's already taken."

Dad crossed his eyes and pushed his false teeth out at me.

The phone woke me one morning. It was Dad. "Someone stole my pants," he said. "Where's my wallet? Can you bring me some money?"

I told him I was loaded, I'd be right over.

"Hurry," he said. "I'm going to see a movie." I couldn't help but grin. Dad didn't just leave the pool hall in his teens; he hadn't stepped inside a movie theater since becoming a Christian more than sixty years ago.

By the time I arrived, he had forgotten why. Seeing me, he said, "What are you doing here? Don't you work?"

I didn't know what else to do, so I laughed.

"I've been out riding the range with Roy Rogers," he said. "We're gonna rope some cattle together. Your mother left me, you know."

Ah, Dad. None of us dreamed it would come to this.

Yesterday, my mother—a woman I have seen share her faith with leather-clad bikers, the girl who led me to Christ when I was a lad—was convinced that God had abandoned her. I was stroking her white hair and singing:

> All the way my Savior leads me
> Oh, the fullness of His love!
> Perfect rest to me is promised
> In my Father's house above.

Suddenly she interrupted me. "No, He didn't." She was indignant.

"You mean Jesus?" I asked.

"He stopped leading me."

"When?" I stammered.

"Last Wednesday."

Doubts come and go. Events of sixty years ago are clearer than the morning news. My mother, once an accomplished writer and my biggest fan, often struggles to finish a four-word sentence. But tonight she is listening to beautiful hymns on a CD player she can't operate and smiling with her eyes closed. "Tell me about the kids," she says.

Dad is concerned that he has misplaced the keys to the car—a car that no longer runs. I tell him they're around here somewhere. I'll find them, don't worry. I can't believe I'm lying to my father. Surely they have manuals for this kind of thing, but I'm learning as I go.

I've brought along a book and I read it to my mother out loud. It is the same tattered copy of *Winnie-the-Pooh* that she read to me when I was four. "How cold my toes...tiddly-pom," I sing using a tune she taught me.

As I leave tonight, I take part again in our grand role reversal, whispering good night to the woman who tucked me in with a thousand good-night kisses.

"God bless you," I say.

"He does," she smiles. "He gave me you."

Then she motions my daughter Rachael to her bedside. "Grandma loves you," she says. "Say it after me so you'll never forget. *Grandma loves me.*"

Rachael smiles and wipes a tear.

Dad is seated in a nearby chair, getting ready for a trip, he says. Going back to Ontario, where he spent his boyhood. Gonna see the tall oak trees and swim in the Elora Gorge. He smiles as he tells me this, and I wonder if it's not the most profound thing he's uttered in years. We're all getting ready for a trip, aren't we? Packing light. Going Home.

Outside, Rachael wants to drive. I can't believe she's already this age. "Will you visit me when I'm old?" I ask, wiping tears and fumbling for the car keys. She smiles her agreement. "I need a hug," I say. She leans close.

Ah yes, I can feel a sneeze coming on.

Alzheimer's Is Limited

It cannot steal the memories I have of you.

It cannot rob the moments we spent laughing together,
Or fade the pictures in my wallet.

Alzheimer's is limited.

It cannot weaken faith.

Deprive me of peace.

Steal my joy.

Or cripple hope.

It cannot shake my confidence that there is a divine plan
though I can't quite see it from here.

Death can take you from me for a time,
  but it cannot steal you away forever.
Alzheimer's is limited.
  It cannot shorten eternal life.
It cannot ruin God's plans for the ultimate family reunion
  Coming one day soon.

37

While I Was Watching

And joy will come again—
warm and secure,
if only for the now,
laughing, we endure.

RUTH BELL GRAHAM

Dear Dad,

We laid you to rest on a Wednesday under the wide Canadian sky. I was hoping for a stray rain cloud to disguise my tears, but I wasn't alone in that department. Saying good-bye to one you've admired since you were knee-high to a tricycle isn't easy. But one who read you bedtime stories? Taught you to ride a bike? And loved you enough to say so? It is positively heartbreaking. Teenagers don't hang out in cemeteries much, but your grandkids refused to leave on Wednesday.

The night before you crossed the River Jordan, they crowded around your bed and sang the hymns you loved to hear. Twice you took my daughter's hand and tried to raise it to your lips. When at last you succeeded in kissing it, she began to weep from sadness and joy and the delight of another memory she'll carry for life.

And that's what you were about, Dad. Memories.

When you thought no one was watching, I learned to laugh. I asked you once what you'd like us to say about you when you're gone. You said with a straight face, "I'd like you to say, 'Look! He's moving!' " But I know you wouldn't trade the riches of eternity for this time-locked place.

When I was a lad, I loved to sneak up on you and watch what you were doing when you didn't know I was there. I don't know that a kid ever adored his dad more than I did.

I saw you smack your thumb with a hammer once, and I held my breath. You danced around using strong language like "Oh shoot!" Then you snickered.

If anyone had reason to cuss, it was you. Your mother died when you were two, leaving you roaming the streets of your hometown alone while your father toiled in a furniture factory. Raised by crazy uncles in a home where the unspeakable was commonplace, you graduated from the school of hard knocks before you entered first grade. But you never shouldered a backpack of grudges. Instead, you warmed our Canadian winters telling stories of a childhood I found enviable, one jammed with fistfights and loaded rifles. You told those stories with a twinkle, too. That twinkle was a way of life for you.

When you thought no one was watching, I learned how to treat a woman. I learned to honor her and open doors for her and when to tip my hat. I learned that we're toast without the ladies, so put them first in line at potlucks. I learned to let them stroll on the inside of the sidewalk so when we're hit by an oncoming truck, they'll still be around to care for the kids.

When you thought no one was watching, I learned what was worth chasing. You avoided the deceptive staircase promising "success," investing in memories instead.

You never owned a new car, but scrounged to buy tent trailers for family vacations.

You blew money on ice cream so we'd stay at the table longer.

You bought flowers for my mother and gifts for my children.

Watching your life, I learned that simplicity is the opposite of simple-mindedness, that those who win the rat race are still rats.

Going through your dresser last night, I found your glasses, heart pills, and a reading lamp. I suspect you're doing fine without them.

You didn't leave much behind. Believe me, we've looked.

In a folder marked "Will," you'd misfiled a note Mom gave you listing your attributes. She made you sound like Father Teresa. "On time for work. A gentleman. Filled with integrity. Wholesome in speech. Loves family. Loves God." I guess it was filed correctly. It's the best inheritance a kid could hope for.

When you thought no one was watching, you showed me how to encourage others. I saw you hug teenagers who had more earrings than brain cells. You smiled and blessed them. Apart from Mom, you were my most boisterous fan, always wanting to applaud my latest book or hear where I was traveling to next. Sometimes now, when I achieve something you would have found significant, it's like I sunk a hole-in-one while golfing by myself.

When you thought no one was watching, I learned how to bring God's Word to life. Hours before you passed away, I had you to myself. You were struggling to breathe, and my singing didn't help, so I told you I loved you and thanked you for being a good dad. Then I opened the same old King James Bible I watched you read when I was a boy. You'd underlined some glorious verses in Revelation 21, and though my voice cracked and quavered, I read them out loud. "And God shall wipe away all tears from their eyes; and there shall be no more death, neither sorrow, nor crying, neither shall there be any more pain: for the former things are passed away." By the time I reached the promise that your name is written in the Lamb's Book of Life, you were sound asleep.

Friday morning the sun rose on your face, and you simply stopped breathing. No more tears. No more Alzheimer's. Home free.

You'll be glad to know your granddaughter Elena braided your comb-over like she'd done a hundred times before. We sat by your bedside, and your daughter, Ruth, said, "Do you suppose he's saved?" And we laughed way too loud—from the deep assurance that you're with Jesus.

Someone said, "I'm sorry you lost your dad," and I said, "Thank you. But how can I say I've lost him when I know exactly where he is?"

When you thought no one was watching, I learned how to die. With relationships intact, with nothing left unsaid.

Four of your five children were there. When we went to tell Mom of your passing, Tim asked, "Do you know why we're here?"

"Money?" said your wife of sixty-two years. You'd have been proud of her.

She held your hand then, clinging to the last of your warmth. For the longest time she didn't say anything, just stared out the window. I asked what she was thinking, and she smiled. "I'd like to take one more stroll in the grass with him." Wouldn't we all? When they came to take you away, she simply said, "Thanks for all the years, sweetheart."

I'd like to thank you too.

Thanks for hunting trips and fishing lessons. Thanks for majoring on the majors. And for a thousand timeless memories. Most of all, thanks for giving me a tiny glimpse of what God looks like.

Tonight I'll lay flowers on your grave once again, and past the tears I'll determine to keep that twinkle alive. To live so the preacher won't have to lie at my funeral. As you cheer me on, all the way Home.

38

The Mailbox

Our lives are shaped by those who love us.
JOHN POWELL

I n seventeen years of writing I have not received anything like the avalanche of mail that descended after I wrote short versions of the previous two chapters for my "Laughing Matters" column. Letters showed up from around the world. Several were from self-described agnostics and atheists—one a childhood friend of mine. Amid generous expletives, he expressed how much he loved being in our home when he was a boy. "Your parents [bad word] loved me when no one else [even badder word] did," the edited version would read.

At least a dozen came from those who had a product guaranteed to fix my Mom. I shall paraphrase what those letters looked like:

Dear Phil,

If you will sign up under me, I believe [enter amazing product here] is the answer to your mother's problems. Since we accepted [enter astoundingly affordable product again] into our lives, we are different people. We have no friends now, but lots of money.

Sincerely,

[enter name here]

One suggested a fascinating therapy. "I manufacture quilts with Bible verses embroidered on them. When spread across their laps, these quilts bring Alzheimer's patients back to us. They are only two hundred dollars each."

Several informed me that it was my fault: "If you just had more faith, she would be healed."

One recommended, "If you can just get her to drink more water every day, she'll be fine."

But mostly, as I pored over these letters, I was struck by people's kindness and compassion. Jeanette Windle, a best-selling novelist, wrote: "Your mother had such an influence on my own life as a writer. I remember vividly being an eighteen-year-old missionary kid lost in the strange, cold country of Canada and reading Bernice Callaway's literature. It gave me hope that one day I would write books too. The rest, of course, is history."

Another author, Maxine Hancock, wrote, "Having just come through the stage you are now in, I know how hard it is: My father lost his mobility, my mother lost her mind, and we came pretty close to losing our sense of humor over the past six years. But both parents have now made it to the Crossing Over point. The losses of old age may be even harder when the contrast between what is and what was is so sharp."

A ninety-one-year-old saint by the name of Delma Jackson told how God had used the story. "I read it many times and it began to dawn on me that while I have eagerly looked forward to going to heaven knowing I am a child of God, I have been in complete denial about this possibility of a 'slow good-bye.' Gradually I began to embrace the fact that if it should come, God would be big enough for even this. The result? A wonderful work of revival is going on in my life. I have been reading His Word and praying that He would help me shine my light in the years I have left."

Vera Tyler of London wrote, "My husband, Bill, died in December after ten years of suffering the increasing confusion and loneliness of Alzheimer's. We watched him lose all memory of the years we spent serving with China Inland Mission, even though he could still speak Chinese. Much of life was forgotten, but he was still praising God and singing the old much-loved hymns. He remained a blessing by being his gracious, grateful self."

Bertha Parker Thompson told me that her mother was the one who knelt with her when she was seven and helped guide her into the family of God. "She also read *Winnie-the-Pooh*. At eighty-six, she has no short-term memory and no logic. She lives on Pop-Tarts and milk, even though she's a diabetic. But she still can sing all the hymns with all the verses. And she can still recite almost all of 'The Cremation of Sam McGee'! Still, we are truly blessed that of all the mothers we could have had, God loaned us to her."

And Sharon McIver-DeBruyn, one of the gals who now refers to my mother as Mom, wrote, "I remember the time I asked my own sweet little mother what she thought about a problem and she replied, 'I don't know. You decide. You are the mother.' It was such a privilege to be my mother's mother as she faded away into that land where she will never grow old. Thank you for this lovely, sensitive reminder that family is so important and God's grace is immeasurable."

The novelist Margaret Lee Runbeck said, "A man leaves all kinds of footprints when he walks through life. Some you can see, like his children and his house. Others are invisible, like the prints he leaves across other people's lives: the help he gives them and what he has said—his jokes, gossip that has hurt others, encouragement. A man doesn't think about it, but everywhere he passes, he leaves some kind of mark."

I once heard someone ask Mom which of her books she was most proud of. I leaned closer at the question, because she had written half a dozen, and I couldn't wait to hear the answer.

"I have five books I'm still working on, and I'm most proud of them," she grinned.

"Oh? And what are the titles?"

"Dave, Dan, Tim, Ruth, and little Philip," she replied. "I hope I'm writing my best material into their lives."

Though I have been privileged to share platforms with some of the greatest orators on Earth, it was my father's words lived out before me that shaped my life far more than any preacher. Though my bookshelves are filled with several thousand volumes of the finest books on faith, it is the life of my mother, a simple farm girl from Ontario, Canada, that has shown me what it means to walk with Christ, how to lean on Him for strength, how to share His joy with others, all the way Home. I thank God for two very human parents who wrote their stories across my life, who taught me early what really mattered. May God give us all strength and wisdom to walk in their steps.

Epilogue

The hand of Jesus is the hand which rules our times.
He regulates our life clock. Christ is for us and Christ is in us.
My times are in His hand.

E. Paxton Hood

A long about the time I conspired to lay this book to rest, my mother sat bolt upright in her hospital bed one evening, smiled widely at me, and asked, "What day is it? Where's Ramona?"

It was like we were in a Sandra Bullock movie and she'd just wakened from a deep coma. I was shocked. Mom, talking in complete sentences.

Thinking it too good to be true, I held up one hand and asked, "How many fingers?"

She laughed. "Seven," she said. "Call a doctor."

Pulling a chair close, I leaned forward as she regaled me with stories long forgotten, naming names I hadn't heard in years. I phoned my brother Dan with the news. "She's even brighter than I," I said.

"I'm sorry to hear that," he joked.

When I told Mom what he had said, she began laughing and hadn't the energy to stop.

Nurses arrived to see if they should give her CPR, and she introduced them to me one by one, without even looking at their nametags. When they left, she whispered, "How much money do I have?"

I told her.

She grinned like she was a child again and was about to dip a schoolmate's pigtails in an inkwell. "Let's give it away," she said.

Months have passed. The blanket near her bed is just a blanket now, no longer her baby. The Bible on her night table lies open; gone is the dust. I am married; no longer am I stealing her money. She grieves her husband's death at times, knowing exactly when it happened, how many months ago, how many days.

Some nights I find her sitting at an old wooden table, writing notes in shaky handwriting—notes to friends and family, encouraging them with a story or a verse from Scripture. "God takes care of me," she often says. "The nurses…they pray with me." And they do. Sometimes I catch them. One whispered, "I'm a Christian. Your mother is such a blessing."

I asked Mom what she would like, seeing as I hadn't given away all her money quite yet.

"I don't know," she said, frowning like she was working on a math equation.

"What about a TV?" I asked.

She shook her head. "Nah. The best years of my life I spent without one." Then her eyes lit up. "Shoes," she said. "I need some shoes."

The next day we decked her in her finest, wedged her into a wheelchair, and went out looking for some. I wish you could have seen her leaving the store with a shoebox on her lap. Her eyes danced, like a four-year-old who has just pulled the wrapping off a Christmas gift she didn't dare dream of receiving.

"Thank you," she kept saying. "Thank you."

I suppose it is the one solitary characteristic that has most endeared her to her children through the years: thanksgiving. This spirit of thanksgiving ensures that several visitors crouch by her bed each day. Thanksgiving helps her focus not on what is missing but what remains. Not on what has taken place but what is yet to come.

Thankful people seem to remember blessings and forget troubles. They are quicker to accept than to analyze, to compliment than to criticize. Helen Keller thanked God for her handicaps. "Through them," she wrote, "I have found myself, my work, and my God."

I don't know too many people who have more to gripe about than Mom. She has broken both hips in separate falls, lost her husband and her hearing and her freedom, yet she cannot find time in her schedule to gripe. It's like she has stepped back a little farther than most of us, seeing the bigger picture, thinking not on what is wrong but on what God is making right. Grateful people don't think less of themselves; they think of themselves less often.

"What are you thankful for today?" I sometimes ask her.

"Oh, so much," she invariably says. "You. And food. I'm getting fat, you know. The food is much too good here. I'm so fat I don't have a lap. I have *laps*."

I guess my mother needs so little, but she needs that little so much. She needs my weekly visits and prayers. She needs updates from her grandchildren and Dad's favorite dog to sit on her laps. She needs a good-night kiss and a kind word and a reminder of the hope we share: the hope of heaven.

These last few years have certainly given me a celestial whiff, a divine desire to count my days, to make the days count. To form each and every decision in light of eternity, mindful that our lives pass quickly but decisions made here last forever.

Thinking on Mom's life, I have found myself saying a more profound prayer than "Help!" the last few days. It is "Thanks."

Thank You, Lord, that the lines have fallen to me in pleasant places. Thank You that You are the God with a history of making all things new, of filling us with hope and joy. And thanks for allowing Your children the last laugh. Verses from Mom's favorite book now open on her night table say it best:

> We know that God, who raised the Lord Jesus, will also raise us with Jesus and present us to himself.... That is why we never give up. Though our bodies are dying, our spirits are being renewed every day. For our present troubles are small and won't last very long. Yet they produce for us a glory that vastly outweighs them and will last forever!... For the things we see now will soon be gone, but the things we cannot see will last forever. (2 Corinthians 4:14, 16–18, NLT)

Notes

1. Tim Stafford, *As Our Years Increase* (Grand Rapids, MI: Zondervan, 1989), 17.

2. T. J. Matthews, Brady E. Hamilton, "American Women Are Waiting to Begin Families," http://www.cdc.gov/nchs/pressroom/02news/ameriwomen.htm (accessed July 29, 2007).

3. U.S. Census Bureau, "Facts for Features," http://www.census.gov/Press-Release/www/releases/archives/facts_for_features_special_editions/006560.html (accessed July 29, 2007).

4. CDC Press Release, "American Women Waiting to Have Families," http://library.adoption.com/parenting-and-families/american-women-waiting-to-begin-families/article/8200/1.html (accessed July 29, 2007).

5. "Sandwich Generation," *Fairlady* magazine, December 2006, http://www.women24.com/Fairlady/Display/FLYArticle/0,,806_11671,00.html (accessed July 29, 2007).

6. Equality and Human Rights Web site, http://www.eoc.org.uk/Default.aspx?page=15440 (accessed July 29, 2007).

7. Charles R. Swindoll, *Growing Wise in Family Life* (Sisters, OR: Multnomah Press, 1988), 152.

8. Ann Rowe Seaman, *America's Most Hated Woman* (Continuum, 2005), 149.

9. I do not have this watch any longer. The watch I wear I got from my grandfather on his deathbed. For twenty bucks, plus tax.

10. Figures are from the Office of National Statistics. (I kid you not. I researched this. You can too!) http://www.dailymail.co.uk/pages/live/femail/article.html?in_article_id=353216&in_page_id=1879 (accessed 10/12/2007)

11. Frederick Buechner, *Wishful Thinking: A Theological ABC* (New York, Harper & Row, 1972), 2.

12. Cheri Fuller, *When Couples Pray: The Little Known Secret to Lifelong Happiness in Marriage* (Sisters, OR: Multnomah, 2001), 12.

13. Cynthia Crossen, "Americans Have It All (But All Isn't Enough)," *The Wall Street Journal*, September 20 1996.

14. "Marriage Brings Wealth, Divorce Steals It" by LiveScience staff posted at, http://www.livescience.com/strangenews/060118_wealth_marriage.html (accessed October 4, 2007).

15. "Limousine Liberal Hypocrisy," *Time* magazine, March 2007, www.time.com/time/magazine/article/0,9171,1599714,00.html (accessed October 10, 2007).

16. Okay, she was not my wife until later, she was my girlfriend…at least, I was hoping she would be.

17. See http://en.wikipedia.org/wiki/Sydney_J._Harris (accessed July 29, 2007).

18. "65 Year Old Woman in India Gives Birth," *FuturePundit,* April 9, 2003, http://www.futurepundit.com/archives/001124.html (accessed October 4, 2007). The case is made all the more remarkable by the fact that the average life expectancy for a female in India is sixty-three.

ACKNOWLEDGMENTS

Without a doubt, this has been the most difficult writing project of my life, and the one I have savored the most. It's nice to live long enough to be nostalgic, but sometimes it hurts. I was startled by the potency of these memories and almost abandoned this project seventy-six times. Along came Ramona who said I could do it, prayed for me each day, and served me lip-smacking lasagna whenever I asked. Behind every good man is a surprised woman. Thanks for your companionship these twenty-five years. I'd do it all again in a heartbeat, minus the time I compared your soup to cardboard. I've said it before: If I knew it would have been this good, I'd have asked you to marry me in third grade.

My editor, Steffany Woolsey, was so encouraging that I have already requested that she and her husband reside next to us in the nursing home beginning in 2041.

The staff at Multnomah was way too kind to me. I sure hope they keep it up.

Thanks to my faithful soldiers of prayer. And the hundreds who filled out my Middle Ages survey. To those who included their names: Your secrets are safe with me.

My high school English teacher, Mr. Al Bienert, looked past my glaring faults and encouraged me. I doubt I'd be writing were it not for him. Al passed away the day I completed this manuscript. He took me to hockey games when I was a student, thus being the only teacher in world history who wanted to spend time with me outside the classroom and therefore my favorite. Mr. Bienert taught me that it's okay to be a kid all your life. I miss him.

I am enormously grateful to my siblings for journeying through this book with me. Only once or twice did we squabble over methods, and once or twice they were right.

God has allowed me to surpass my legal limit in friends, each of whom used more of their shoulders than their mouths during the last few years. I am blessed to know each one, and humbled by several when we golf.

Thanks also to my children, two guys and a girl who travel with me, pray with me, and allow me to write about them. Perhaps they keep thinking I'll strike it rich. With kids like these, I already have. Come home anytime. Mom's making lasagna.

All praise and honor to my Savior Jesus Christ, who loved me and gave Himself for me. A lifetime is far too short to sing Your praise.

ABOUT THE AUTHOR

Phil Callaway is president of Laugh Again Ministries, an award-winning humorist, best-selling author, and the only one we know who broke his nose dropping barbells in ninth grade. About a hundred times a year, Callaway brings his humor with a message to corporations, conferences, and churches. Phil is the author of *Laughing Matters, It's Always Darkest Before the Fridge Door Opens,* and *Parenting: Don't Try This At Home,* and his writings have been translated into languages like Spanish, Polish, Chinese, and English—one of which he speaks fluently. His five-part video series, *The Big Picture,* has been viewed in eighty thousand churches worldwide. Phil is married to his high school sweetheart, Ramona. They live in Canada. For more information on Phil's other books, CDs, DVDs, or speaking ministry, visit www.laughagain.org or write Laugh and Learn, P.O. Box 4576, Three Hills, AB T0M 2N0.

෧෨

Phil is editor of *Servant* magazine, an award-winning magazine read in 101 countries. A ministry of Prairie Bible College, *Servant* is full of insightful interviews with well-known Christians, helpful articles, world news, and Phil's trademark humor. For a complimentary one-year subscription, please call 1-800-221-8532, or write:

Servant Magazine
Box 4000
Three Hills, AB Canada
T0M 2N0

Learning to Laugh When Life Stinks

Sometimes life just stinks. People disappoint. Bad things happen. Hardship comes in double helpings. The last thing you want to do is laugh. So let hilarious humorist Phil Callaway show you—as only he can—that some of the darkest times are those just before the fridge door opens.